First World War
and Army of Occupation
War Diary
France, Belgium and Germany

59 DIVISION
Divisional Troops
Royal Army Veterinary Corps
59 Mobile Veterinary Section
1 January 1917 - 28 April 1919

WO95/3019/2

The Naval & Military Press Ltd
www.nmarchive.com
Published in association with The National Archives

Published by

The Naval & Military Press Ltd

Unit 10 Ridgewood Industrial Park,

Uckfield, East Sussex,

TN22 5QE England

Tel: +44 (0) 1825 749494

www.naval-military-press.com

www.nmarchive.com

This diary has been reprinted in facsimile from the original. Any imperfections are inevitably reproduced and the quality may fall short of modern type and cartographic standards.

© Crown Copyright
Images reproduced by permission of The National Archives, London, England, 2015.

Contents

Document type	Place/Title	Date From	Date To
Heading	WO95/3019/2 59 Mobile Veterinary Sector		
War Diary	Station Vevormany Hospital Kildade	01/01/1917	01/01/1917
War Diary	Ireland	02/01/1917	11/01/1917
War Diary	The Barracks Kildendt Ireland	12/01/1917	17/01/1917
War Diary	Curragh	17/01/1917	17/01/1917
War Diary	Dublin	17/01/1917	17/01/1917
War Diary	Liverpool	18/01/1917	18/01/1917
War Diary	Amesbury	18/01/1917	19/01/1917
War Diary	Larkhill	20/01/1917	21/01/1917
War Diary	No 18 camp larhill	22/01/1917	31/01/1917
War Diary	No 18 Camp Larkhill Salisbury	01/02/1917	28/02/1917
War Diary	No 18 Camp Larkhill Salisbury	01/02/1917	18/02/1917
War Diary	Southampton	19/02/1917	22/02/1917
War Diary	Le Havre	23/02/1917	23/02/1917
War Diary	Longueau	24/02/1917	27/02/1917
War Diary	Mericourt Sur Somme	28/02/1917	09/03/1917
War Diary	Proyart	10/03/1917	29/03/1917
War Diary	Mons-En Chaussee	30/03/1917	31/03/1917
War Diary	In The Field	01/03/1917	30/04/1917
Miscellaneous	DAG 3rd Echelon		
War Diary	In The Field	01/05/1917	31/07/1917
War Diary	Purquegny	01/08/1917	23/08/1917
War Diary	Bouzincourt	24/08/1917	31/08/1917
War Diary	In Train	01/09/1917	01/09/1917
War Diary	Winnezeele	02/09/1917	24/09/1917
War Diary	Brandhoek	25/09/1917	02/10/1917
War Diary	Steenbecque	03/10/1917	06/10/1917
War Diary	Pufuginy	07/10/1917	14/10/1917
War Diary	Petil Serisnd	15/10/1917	28/10/1917
War Diary	Barlin	29/10/1917	17/11/1917
War Diary	Humeroeville	18/11/1917	19/11/1917
War Diary	Basseux	20/11/1917	24/11/1917
War Diary	Etricourt	25/11/1917	03/12/1917
War Diary	Havrincourt Wood	04/12/1917	17/12/1917
War Diary	Leavuvilli	18/12/1917	31/12/1917
War Diary	Le Cauroy	01/01/1918	09/02/1918
War Diary	Monchest	10/02/1918	10/02/1918
War Diary	Envellers	11/02/1918	21/03/1918
War Diary	Ayette	23/03/1918	23/03/1918
War Diary	Bouzencourt	24/03/1918	26/03/1918
War Diary	Frenvillers	27/03/1918	29/03/1918
War Diary	Hungoual	30/03/1918	31/03/1918
War Diary	Equedecques	01/04/1918	01/04/1918
War Diary	Hurbecque	02/04/1918	02/04/1918
War Diary	Proven Road	03/04/1918	07/04/1918
War Diary	Bronehoek	08/04/1918	13/04/1918
War Diary	Abeele	14/04/1918	19/04/1918
War Diary	St Sixte	20/04/1918	21/04/1918
War Diary	Bambecque	22/04/1918	12/05/1918
War Diary	Eps	13/05/1918	17/05/1918

War Diary	Dieval	18/05/1918	31/05/1918
War Diary	In The Field	01/06/1918	30/06/1918
War Diary	Bomy	01/07/1918	11/07/1918
War Diary	Monchy Cayeux	12/07/1918	26/07/1918
War Diary	Basseux	27/07/1918	25/08/1918
War Diary	Norrent Fontes	26/08/1918	28/08/1918
War Diary	Treizennes	29/08/1918	31/08/1918
War Diary	O18 a 2.8 Sheet 36 A Guarbecque	01/09/1918	06/09/1918
War Diary	Haystack Farm	07/09/1918	14/09/1918
War Diary	Q 19a.6.0. Sheet 36a Haystack Farm	15/09/1918	04/10/1918
War Diary	Estairs-Neufberquin Road	05/10/1918	10/10/1918
War Diary	G17 Central Sheet 36	11/10/1918	20/10/1918
War Diary	G20b5.8 Hem	21/10/1918	31/10/1918
War Diary	G20 65.8 Sheet 37 Hem	01/11/1918	10/11/1918
War Diary	Sheet 37. H.17 d 3.2 Bailleul	11/11/1918	16/11/1918
War Diary	V29 Of 9.5 Sheet 36 Seglin	17/11/1918	30/11/1918
War Diary	Seclin	01/12/1918	05/12/1918
War Diary	Barlin	06/12/1918	09/03/1919
War Diary	Balinghem	10/03/1919	28/04/1919
Heading	59th Division 59th Divisional Train Feb 1917-Aug 1919 (513 To 516 08c) And 1916 Jan-1916 Jun		

WO95/30019/2

5ª Mobile Veterinary Section

Army Form C. 2118.

WAR DIARY
or
INTELLIGENCE SUMMARY.
(Erase heading not required.)

Jany 1917 — 2/1 N.M. M.V.S — 59th Division.

Instructions regarding War Diaries and Intelligence Summaries are contained in F. S. Regs., Part II. and the Staff Manual respectively. Title pages will be prepared in manuscript.

28 MAY 1919

Place	Date	Hour	Summary of Events and Information	Remarks and references to Appendices
Stephen Esplanade Hospital, 1, FILDAS, IRELAND	Jany 1/17		General Routine	
"	Jan 2		General Routine	
"	Jan 3		General Routine	
"	Jan 4		Advanced Party of the R.C.O.S 2 Yrs. Arrived to FOVANT SALISBURY PLAIN	
"	Jan 5		Preparations taken in hand for move to SALISBURY PLAIN	
"	Jan 6		Nothing to report	
"	Jan 7		63rd Divisional mobile Veterinary Section arrive	
"	Jan 8		Checking of Stores to be handed over to 63rd M.V.S.	
"	Jan 9		2nd Advance Party of the R.C.O.S 2 Yrs proceeds to CHELMSFORD to take over Mobilization Stores	
"	"		2/1 & 4 M.V.S.	
"	Jan 10		General Routine	
"	Jan 11		Stores, Veterinary dispatched taken over by 63rd M.V.S. from 2/3rd M.V.S from M.V.S.	
"	"		Nothing to report	
"	Jan 12		" "	
"	Jan 13		" "	
"	Jan 14		" "	
"	Jan 15		" "	

WAR DIARY
or
INTELLIGENCE SUMMARY.
(Erase heading not required.)

Army Form C. 2118.

Place	Date	Hour	Summary of Events and Information	Remarks and references to Appendices
N. Barracks KILDARE	16/1/17		Final preparations for move to England made	
	17/1/17	8.0.a.m.	Proceed to Curragh Sidings	
CURRAGH	17/1/17	9.0.a.m.	Entrain Horses & Vehicles	
	17/1/17	10.30 a.m.	Train moves off for DUBLIN	
	17/1/17	12.30 p.m.	Arrive North Wall DUBLIN	
DUBLIN	17/1/17	2.0 p.m.	Commence Embarkation Vehicles & Horses on board H.M.S. Slieve	
	17/1/17	7.30 p.m.	H.M.S. Slieve departs	
LIVERPOOL	18/1/17	4.30 a.m.	Arrive Liverpool	
	18/1/17	9.0 a.m.	Disembark vehicles. Section assists in the disembarkation of all the remounts on board	
	18/1/17	10.0 a.m.	Vehicles & Remounts entrained at Pier & sent Station	
	18/1/17 No: N 12.15		Train moves off en route for AMESBURY	
AMESBURY	19/1/17	10.30 p.m.	Arrive AMESBURY Commence discentrain	
	20/1/17	1.0. a.m.	Proceed to No 6 Camp LARKHILL	
LARKHILL	20/1/17		General Routine	
	21/1/17		General Routine	

Army Form C. 2118.

WAR DIARY
or
INTELLIGENCE SUMMARY.
(Erase heading not required.)

Instructions regarding War Diaries and Intelligence Summaries are contained in F. S. Regs., Part II. and the Staff Manual respectively. Title pages will be prepared in manuscript.

Place	Date	Hour	Summary of Events and Information	Remarks and references to Appendices
to R Camp EARHILL	22/1/17		Proposed leaves taken in lieu of that overseas	
"	23/1/17		Routine duties	
"	24/1/17		"	
"	25/1/17		Other ranks proceed on overseas embarkation leave	
"	26/1/17		Routine duties	
"	27/1/17		"	
"	28/1/17		"	
"	29/1/17		"	
"	30/1/17		"	
"	31/1/17		"	
"	3/1/17		"	

W.T. Morgan Major
for O.C. 21(N.M.)M.V.S.

Army Form C. 2118.

WAR DIARY
or
INTELLIGENCE SUMMARY

59 Div.
Mobile Vety. Sect.
Feb. 1917
Vol I

(Erase heading not required.)

Instructions regarding War Diaries and Intelligence Summaries are contained in F. S. Regs., Part II and the Staff Manual respectively. Title Pages will be prepared in manuscript.

Place	Date 1917	Hour	Summary of Events and Information	Remarks and references to Appendices
Rushall Camp	Feb 1	6 p.m.	Shelter, water and filling of straw. Issuing Serum. Issuing of firearms. Inoculation and hair clipping.	
	2		Shelter, watering & feeding of Horses. Examining & passing of sick horses taking charge of Convalescent & sick horses generally. Demobilisation of 012.	
	3		Capt Smith and 9 other ranks go on leave this evening. Additional bedding issue to 012	
Larkhill	4		do	
	5		do	
	6		Admitted 16 Dangerous Infectious outlying from Gas poisoning (Rivington Camp) for examination. No 22,23,24. Received. 2. General Rembled for west to A? Horses inoculated at A.V.H. 59th Division. Pte Cook reported slightly injured from Cart.	
	7		do	Pte Cook, Contusion examined. O/C and 9 Other Ranks return from leave.
	8		do	
	9		do	do. 9 more admit Gas Cases etc.
	10		do	do. 8 Other Ranks go on leave.
	11		do	
	12		do	do. Rifle drill.
	13		do	
	14		do	do. Kit inspection by O/C.
	15		do	do. 8 Other Ranks return from leave. O/C made enquiries on the spot.
	16		do	Pte Banks discharged from Hospital. Inoculations for overseas service.
	17		do	do. Final from O/C Details completed between 1 & 4 p.m.
	18		do	do. Arrangements completed for home. Regimental handovers to 59 details to complete and trans pack amounts to amusement taken forthwith to 14/15 Southampton armies Southampton Docks.
	19		do	Boat amrnd? Details arranged on board ship to Southampton armies.
	20		do	Transport jammed in the harbour followed [...] transport to Boat lines 5.30 pm

Army Form C. 2118.

WAR DIARY
or
INTELLIGENCE SUMMARY

(Erase heading not required.)

Instructions regarding War Diaries and Intelligence Summaries are contained in F. S. Regs., Part II. and the Staff Manual respectively. Title Pages will be prepared in manuscript.

Place	Date	Hour	Summary of Events and Information	Remarks and references to Appendices
	1917 July 21		Road survey of the Ecole Rondbourier for Brig. 2 i/c & who joined 74th on arrival for duty.	
	22		Arrived at Havre 3. 4.15 a.m. and disembarked. March to 2nd Rest Camp for night.	
	23		Leave le Havre by rail at 10.30 a.m. for Perrignean.	
	24		Arrive Perrignean at 4.0 a.m. and march to Billets.	
	25		Await instructions for move.	
	26		Receive instructions to move on 27th instead to Rouxmesnil Sur Sonne	
	27		Leave Perrignean with Divisional Head Quarters for Rouxmesnil Sur Sonne arrive 5 p.m.	
	28		General Rawlinson O/C visits Batt. Cracking Brook.	

Guy G Postly
Capt & O.i/c
OMC
2/1 R. Rutland Mobile Vety Section

Army Form C. 2118.

21st NORTH MIDLAND MOBILE VETERINARY SECTION

WAR DIARY
or
INTELLIGENCE SUMMARY.
(Erase heading not required.)

Instructions regarding War Diaries and Intelligence Summaries are contained in F.S. Regs., Part II. and the Staff Manual respectively. Title pages will be prepared in manuscript.

Place	Date	Hour	Summary of Events and Information	Remarks and references to Appendices
No. 18 Camp LARKHILL SALISBURY	1/2/17		Stables. Watering and feeding of Horses. Grooming. Exercise. Dressing of Sick Horses. Lecture	
do	2/2/17		Stables. Watering and feeding of Horses. Grooming. Exercise. Dressing of Sick Horses. Lecture by Lt Colonel [illegible]	
do	3/2/17		General Routine	
do	4/2/17		General Routine	
do	5/2/17		Visit the A.D.V.S. Col. BURRIN at CANARD SALISBURY for instructions. Rec'd 7 sick H's	
do			into open shed. Bure Finla with the 6th suffering from Gas Poisoning	
do	12/2/17		General Routine. A.D.V.S. Col. BURRIN visited section.	
do	13/2/17		General Routine Recv'd 2 H's sick from Gun Section	
do	14/2/17		General Routine	
do		2 pm	Route March on foot	
do	15/2/17		General Routine	
do	16/2/17		General Routine	
do	17/2/17		Recv'd 1 Routine	
do	18/2/17		Riding Exercise in [illegible] etc	
do	19/2/17		3 Other Ranks returned from leave	
do	20/2/17		[illegible] sent out [illegible] Horse Hospital. [illegible]	

1/1 NORTH MIDLAND MOBILE VETERINARY SECTION

Army Form C. 2118.

WAR DIARY
or
INTELLIGENCE SUMMARY.
(Erase heading not required.)

Instructions regarding War Diaries and Intelligence Summaries are contained in F. S. Regs., Part II. and the Staff Manual respectively. Title pages will be prepared in manuscript.

Place	Date	Hour	Summary of Events and Information	Remarks and references to Appendices
TOTON CAMP LONGMOOR SALISBURY PL.	1/2/17		Visit of 2/Lt Detmold re completion of Stores	
do	7/2/17		Arrangements completed for move. Advance party handed over to 2/Lt Detmold	
	8/9/17 10-40		Used entrains at AYLESBURY en route for SOUTHAMPTON	
	9/2/17 12-0		Arrive SOUTHAMPTON DOCKS	
SOUTHAMPTON	10/2/17		Horses exercised	
	10/2/17 9.30		Embark on H.M.S. NORTH WESTERN MILLER	
	10/2/17 11-30		Boat moves out	
	11/2/17		Boat hung up in COWES ROADS owing to fog	
	11/2/17 7.0pm		Boat leaves and moves off to France	
	12/2/17 7.0pm		Arrive LE HAVRE & disembark. Proceed to tie & Rest Camp for night	
LE HAVRE	13/2/17 12 noon		Entrain en route for LONGUEAU, SOMME	
LONGUEAU	14/2/17 4.30am		Arrive & detrain	
do	15/2/17		Awaiting instructions	
do	16/2/17		Receive instructions to move to MERICOURT-SUR-SOMME on 27 inst	
	27/2/17		Proceed with Personnel Headquarters to MERICOURT-SUR-SOMME	
MERICOURT-SUR-SOMME	28/2/17		General Routine.	

Capt OC
F 1/1 N M Mobile Veterinary Section

… NORTH MIDLAND MOBILE VETERINARY SECTION

WAR DIARY
or
INTELLIGENCE SUMMARY.
(Erase heading not required.)

Army Form C. 2118.

Place	Date	Hour	Summary of Events and Information	Remarks and references to Appendices
MORCOURT SUR-SOMME	1/3/17		Genl and Routine. Capt Scales over to Sub HQrs at MORCOURT	
	2/3/17		Lt Col Schy goes to BAYONNE VILLERS LONGUEAU & SALEUX	
do	3/3/17		Inspection of Sick Horses at MORCOURT	
do	4/3/17		Capt Schy over to watch Vetny Section at BRAY and also to see Lt Col Barker	
do	5/3/17		General Routine. Gas Helmet inspection. Horses inspected & measured CC	
do	6/3/17		General Routine. Capt Schy over to BRAY re Vetny Sec. got new Horses	
do	7/3/17		Routine. Gas Helmet inspection. Box Respirators explained	
do	8/3/17		General Routine	
do	9/3/17		General to PROYART	
PROYART	10/3/17		General Routine. Capt Schy inspects all horses at MORCOURT. Sub HQrs also inspected by General	
do	11/3/17		General Routine	
do	12/3/17		General Routine. Visit of A.D.V.S. 30th Div	
do	13/3/17		Capt Schy inspects Sick horses at MORCOURT & MERICOURT-SUR-SOMME	
do	14/3/17		General Routine. Capt Schy milllent horses of Section	
do	15/3/17		General Routine. Visit from A.D.V.S. 30th Div	
do	16/3/17		Capt Schy to MERICOURT-SUR-SOMME to see Sick horses of NMDA	

2/1st NORTH MIDLAND MOBILE VETERINARY SECTION

Army Form C. 2118.

WAR DIARY or INTELLIGENCE SUMMARY.
(Erase heading not required.)

Instructions regarding War Diaries and Intelligence Summaries are contained in F. S. Regs., Part II. and the Staff Manual respectively. Title pages will be prepared in manuscript.

Place	Date	Hour	Summary of Events and Information	Remarks and references to Appendices
PRAYART	17/3/17		General Routine. Capt Bailey goes to Remount Depot near	
"	18/3/17		Follow our Instructors to FAVREUIL R.P. to draw 60 sick horses	
"	19/3/17		General Routine	
"	20/3/17		Horses evacuated to 21 Aux Base Veterinary Hospital	
"	21/3/17		General Routine	
"	22/3/17		Collect our horses sent to ESTREES EN SAPIGNY	
"	23/3/17		General Routine	
"	24/3/17		General Routine. Visit of A.D.V.S. 39 to Div	
"	25/3/17		Party sent to MERICOURT CURSEOURT to collect sick horses 37 D.W.R.s	
"	26/3/17		General Routine. A.D.V.S. 39 to Div visits Section for inspection	
"	27/3/17		Horses evacuated to No. 4 Veterinary Hospital	
"	28/3/17		General Routine. Instructor Horse received for transfer to Vet 1. DHALSHZ	
"	29/3/17		Transit to ST CHRIST en route for WIENS EN CHAUSSEE	
MONS EN CHAUSSEE	30/3/17		Routine MONS EN CHAUSSEE	
"	31/3/17		General Routine. Party sent to St Christ to collect sick horses	

Army Form C. 2118

WAR DIARY
or
INTELLIGENCE SUMMARY
(Erase heading not required.)

Instructions regarding War Diaries and Intelligence Summaries are contained in F. S. Regs., Part II. and the Staff Manual respectively. Title Pages will be prepared in manuscript.

Place	Date	Hour	Summary of Events and Information	Remarks and references to Appendices
Q.H. Judd	2/3/17	6.30am / to 5.30	General Routine. Lieut. Corby goes by motor car to see Lieut. Morris	
	3/3/17		Lieut Corby goes to Bayonvilliers, Fouquescourt and Onbuy. Inspection of Lieut Morris at moment.	
	4/3/17		Lieut Corby goes to H.Q. and round, & also to 246 Cushier.	
	5/3/17		General Routine on a big difficult instalment. Prendelets but difficulties and arrears for internment.	
	6/3/17		Lewin Chaptal. Capt. Corby goes to Bayne Quarters for horses on train.	
	7/3/17		General Routine. Gas incident inspection. Box Respirators extend.	
	8/3/17		General Routine. Nothing except and Chis duel.	
	9/3/17		Move to Proyart and take up Quarters there.	
	10/3/17		General Routine. Capt Lovelogino to 2nd round to watch horses of no. 3/94 Col. R.A.C. Stabled at new Quarters also pieces blanks	
	11/3/17		General Routine.	
	12/3/17		General Routine. Visit from A.D.V.S. afternoon	
	13/3/17		Especial Roys Gun. Capt Corby visits Lieut Morris at B moment?	
	14/3/17		General Routine.	
	15/3/17		Capt Corby auditions horses at Lieut Lewin Chaplain. Visit from A.D.V.S. afternoon	

WAR DIARY or INTELLIGENCE SUMMARY

Army Form C. 2118

March 1917

Mobile Vet. Section

Vol 2

Place	Date	Hour	Summary of Events and Information	Remarks and references to Appendices
In the Field	16/3/17	6.30 am / 3.30 pm	General Routine. N.C.O. sent to hurricane. Gun. Servant to our sick horse 17 Wind Quarters	
	17/3/17		General Routine. Cpl & Cook Orderly to Headquarters	
	18/3/17		General Routine. Collecting fatigue and 6 Government to bury in the R Miraus	
	19/3/17		General Routine. Ns. J.C. took R. to M. C. 2 Bre to Hospital, evacuated by Bray Cleary Station	
	20/3/17		Party sent to Bray Hospital with Horses for Evacuation	
	21/3/17		General Routine	
	22/3/17		Party sent to Estrus. Party sent to Bras Hospital when Evacuated	
	23/3/17		General Routine	
	24/3/17		General Routine. Transferred to P.O.L. Syth Division	
	25/3/17		Party sent to sick convoy. Sun. Command to remove sick Horse belonging to Head Quarters	
	26/3/17		General Routine. April 5 S.E. Command notice to move for Evacuation	
	27/3/17		Party sent to Bras Veterinary Hospital with Horses for Evacuation	
	28/3/17		General Routine. Instruction received to move to Sonne en Chausee	
	29/3/17		Move to St Chrus envious for Horses en Chausee	
	30/3/17		Same St Chrus for moves en Chausee and take at Quaden thir	
	31/3/17		General Routine. Party sent to St Chrus to collect sick Hy: oft Gud animals	

Sig. J Scott
Capt A.V.C.
O/C

WAR DIARY or INTELLIGENCE SUMMARY

Army Form C. 2118

2/1st N. Midland Mobile Veterinary Section
2nd Division

Place	Date	Hour	Summary of Events and Information	Remarks and references to Appendices
Y.M.C 2/Lt	1/4/17		Lieut A R Munrose Horse Ambulance goes to Tracing for the Sick Horses visit from depot.	
	2/4/17		Horse Ambulance visits town for A.S.C.	
	3/4/17		Cap.t Crosby goes with A.D.v.S. at depot to see Sick Horses, not to arrange for evacuation of same.	
	4/4/17		11 Horses of "B" Echelon A.V.C. 29th Division admitted to sick horse station	
	5/4/17		4 Horses wounded to base to Veterinary Hospital, 2 other with 11 A.V.C. (K-013 Coy) Horse.	
	6/4/17		Horses 9 Cook R.20.29 & 38c horses no leg on the journey from horse evacuated to hospital. Arrived to Mobile Veterinary Station for evacuation to England.	
	7/4/17		Heard from 6/04/17 29th Division Evil Chicken on & 3 other horses go to Depot. Commencement Horses for Evacuation	
	8/4/17		Ambulance visited Sick Horse from 469 Coy. R E at Belleville Farm.	
	9/4/17		Heard from A.D.v.S. Service routine	
	10/4/17		Evil and Routine. Nothing unusual.	
	11/4/17		Evil Chickens on returned with Ambulance.	
	12/4/17		1 Horse admitted to Sick Horse. Capt Crosby and 10 men goes two horses from Depot from Hospital La Paque with 29 horses for evacuation.	
	13/4/17		Capt Crosby 13 min return from La Paque. Veterinary day Casualty 29 horses. No epizootic diseases.	

Army Form C. 2118

WAR DIARY
or
INTELLIGENCE SUMMARY
(Erase heading not required.)

Instructions regarding War Diaries and Intelligence Summaries are contained in F. S. Regs., Part II. and the Staff Manual respectively. Title Pages will be prepared in manuscript.

Unit: 2nd/1st Northern Veterinary Section
59th Division

Place	Date	Hour	Summary of Events and Information	Remarks and references to Appendices
South Nutfield	15/4/17		Cpl L Foster ill and men 39 & 43 provide Escort and supply escort for evacuation. 14 men and 39 horses admitted to Divisional Horse Rest Camp (attd 59th Divl R.Con) 2 & 3.	
	16/4/17		40 Dowson PC, Jr Cook reports from 1st E.Base to him any Hospital [Forage].	
	17/4/17		Capt Conty inspects Horses of 428 Coy (2 Pieces) R.E. at E. Catels.	
	18/4/17		Visit from A.D.V.S. Nothing unusual to-day.	
	19/4/17		General Routine.	
	20/4/17		General Routine.	
	21/4/17		Capt Conty goes to Billing Cathenil & Ambroise, inspects horses belonging to 243 Field Ambulance	
	22/4/17		Capt Conty goes to Billing Cathenil and by Motor to 200 Machine Gun Coy at Beaumetz.	
	23/4/17		General Routine	
	24/4/17		Capt Dowson inspects horses at Le Catelet.	
	25/4/17		General Routine. Capt Conty goes to Pressoir Cadeau Ypres	
	26/4/17		General Routine. Sergt A Wickett. I.E. 416 Reports for duty.	
	27/4/17		Visit from A.D.V.S.	
	28/4/17		Visit from D.D.V.S. Fourth Army.	
	29/4/17		24 Horses Evacuation to Base Veterinary Hospital.	
	30/4/17		General Routine.	

2 Men & Three Ambulances received three Sick Horses from Divisional I.A.C.C. & 3 men transferred to III Corps Mobile Veterinary Department.

R J Scott
Lieut
Capt N.V.S.
½

D.A.G.
3rd Echelon
Le Bassy.

156

Herewith please war diary for the month of May.

Guy D Westby
Capt. AVC
O/C
2/1 N. Midland Mobile Vety
Section
59th Division

June 4/7.

WAR DIARY or INTELLIGENCE SUMMARY

Army Form C. 2118

MOB Vety Sec.

(Erase heading not required.)

Instructions regarding War Diaries and Intelligence Summaries are contained in F. S. Regs., Part II. and the Staff Manual respectively. Title Pages will be prepared in manuscript.

Place	Date	Hour	Summary of Events and Information	Remarks and references to Appendices
In the field	1/5/17		26 Horses evacuated to Base Veterinary Hospital Ayges les Bains	
	2/5/17		6 Stallhamed of Horses of Section relieved by Lire	
	3/5/17		Capt Sorby goes to Beauvoir to inspect forde of 500 & horshow gun Section	
	4/5/17		Sick Horses removed in Ambulance from Bouronville & Rousel. ADVS 54th Div. vis. Vet. Section	
	5/5/17		General Roustan, Capt Sorby goes to V/S conference	
	6/5/17		Sick Horses removed in ambulance from Vrocnis & Rousel	
	7/5/17		General Roustan	
	8/5/17		Visit of DDVS 4th Army. General Roustan	
	9/5/17		18 Horses evacuated. ADS Veterinary Hospital forges les Eaux	
	10/5/17		General Roustan. Visit of ADVS 54th Div. Horses removed in Ambulance from Tunterry & Vares	
	11/5/17		Horses removed from Tincourt in Ambulance. General Roustan	
	12/5/17		24 Horses evacuated to Hospital and in the M.V. S. Car's	
	13/5/17		6 Horses evacuated to Veterinary Hospital forges les Eaux	
	14/5/17		General Roustan	
	15/5/17		Horses removed from Cartigny in Ambulance	
	16/5/17		7 Horses evacuated to Veterinary Hospital forges les Eaux. Visit of ADVS 54th Div	
	17/5/17		2 Horses removed in Ambulance from Hamelet	

Army Form C. 2118.

WAR DIARY
or
INTELLIGENCE SUMMARY

(Erase heading not required.)

Army Veterinary Service
57th Div

Place	Date	Hour	Summary of Events and Information	Remarks and references to Appendices
In the Field	17/5/17		Visit of O.D.V.S. to Army. Horse removed in Ambulance from Berves	
	18/5/17		Capt Sowby goes to 2/1st conference	
	19/5/17		1 Corps & 3 Ptes return for duty from III Corps Mobile Veterinary Department	
	20/5/17		Horse removed from Bomely in Ambulance	
	21/5/17		General Routine	
	22/5/17		19 Horses evacuated to a Veterinary Hospital Forges Les Eaux	
	23/5/17		General Routine	
	24/5/17		General Routine, Capt Sowby goes to V/O conference	
	25/5/17		General Routine	
	26/5/17		13 Horses evacuated to Veterinary Hospital	
	27/5/17		Horse removed in Ambulance from Vracines	
	28/5/17		General Routine	
	29/5/17		11 Horses evacuated to Veterinary Hospital Forges Les Eaux	
	30/5/17		General Routine	
	31/5/17		General Routine	

SECRET   Army Form C. 2118.

WAR DIARY
or
INTELLIGENCE SUMMARY
(Erase heading not required.)

2/ N. Mid. Mob. Vet Section   Vol 5

Place	Date	Hour	Summary of Events and Information	Remarks and references to Appendices
In the Field	1/6/17		Mob Vet Section moves to Epinencourt	
	2/6/17		General Routine nothing unusual to report	
	3/6/17		General Routine	
	4/6/17		General Routine Gas Alarm 11.30 p.m.	
	5/6/17		General Routine No. 7702 3987 LingL.G. admitted with Hospital	
	6/6/17		Horse Ambulance brings in 2 Horses from 125 & Batt R.G.A.	
	7/6/17		Sergt Marshall goes to Abbeville with 2 sick Horses and 2 Horses to Vet Hosp. Rail	
	8/6/17		Horse Ambulance sent for horses from 116 Bde R.G.A.	
	9/6/17		35 Horses evacuated from Sections to Rouge Veterinary Hospital	
	10/6/17		General Routine	
	11/6/17		General Routine	
	12/6/17		2.C.O. & Men return from Base Veterinary Hospital	
	13/6/17		Capt Brothy meets D.A.G.V. to inspect horses also to 62nd Labour Batt to see sick horses	
	14/6/17		Capt Brothy visits 62nd Labour Batt to see sick Horses	
	15/6/17		General Routine	
	16/6/17		No 7703 TO2 397 returns to Unit from Hospital	
			15 Horses 2 Mules evacuated from Sections to Base Veterinary Hospital	
	17/6/17		Horse Ambulance sent to Signal Coy R.E. for Sick Horse	
	18/6/17		General Routine	
	19/6/17		General Routine	
	20/6/17		General Routine a visit from A.D.V.S. sgn Res	
	21/6/17		General Routine Capt Brothy visits field Cashier at C4 recount	
	22/6/17		General Routine free of their Gonel	

WAR DIARY or INTELLIGENCE SUMMARY

Army Form C. 2118.

Place	Date	Hour	Summary of Events and Information	Remarks and references to Appendices
In the Field	23/6/17		21 Horses evacuated from Section to Base Veterinary Hospital	
	24/6/17		General Routine	
	25/6/17		General Routine. W.C.O & 2 men return from Base Hospital	
	26/6/17		Ambulance sent for Horse from 125 H.Row. R.G.A.	
	27/6/17		Horse Ambulance removes Horses from A 181 Battery to 51st D in Mobile Vet Section	
			Capt. Roxby Maude 110 Heavy Battery % McClain Horses	
			Capt Roxby visits 115 Heavy Battery R.G.A. % McClain Horses	
	28/6/17		Capt Roxby Makes Veterinary Charge of 178 Brigade and visits this Unit & 200 "H.G.Rey	
	29/6/17		General Routine	
	30/6/17		General Routine	

Guy Roxby
Capt Roxby
% 1/1 N Midlds Veterinary Section
2/1/1 N Midlds Veterinary Section

WAR DIARY or INTELLIGENCE SUMMARY

2/1st N. Midland Veterinary Section

Instructions regarding War Diaries and Intelligence Summaries are contained in F. S. Regs., Part II. and the Staff Manual respectively. Title Pages will be prepared in manuscript.

Army Form C. 2118.

Place	Date	Hour	Summary of Events and Information	Remarks and references to Appendices
In the Field	1/7/17		Ambulance sent for sick horse	
	2/7/17		Ambulance sent. 179 Howitzer Group cops. for sick horse	
	3/7/17		Eleven animals evacuated to Base Veterinary Hospital	
	4/7/17		Capt Scott inspects horses of Shenwood Foresters & 200 Br. G.A.	
	5/7/17		General Routine	
	6/7/17		General Routine, insp. of D.A.D.V.S. 59th Div	
	7/7/17		Further animals evacuated to Base Veterinary Hospital	
	8/7/17		General Routine	
	9/7/17		Capt Scott goes on leave	
	10/7/17		Lieutenant Vaughey for this evening sent No.1723911 Pt Sergt. S. Yves on leave	
	11/7/17		Section takes up quarters at Rougigny	
	12/7/17		Visit from D.A.D.V.S. 59th Div.	
	13/7/17		" "	
	14/7/17		Inspection of Small Kit Saddlery & Buckets by Capt Davies A.V.C.	
	15/7/17		Inspection of Horses, Shoes + Clothing by D.A.D.V.S.	
	16/7/17		General Return	
	17/7/17		Twelve animals evacuated to Base Veterinary Hospital	
	18/7/17		General Routine. Visit from D.O.D. 10. V.S 59th Div	
	19/7/17		Divisional Sports	
	20/7/17		General Routine. Sergt Prentice reports for duty	
	21/7/17		Divisional Sports	
	22/7/17		Inspection of Saddlery + Horses by D.A.D.V.S. 59 Div. No.170 T.O.2422 Cpl Wilkinson reported 2/1st Field Ambulance in connection with the laundry of horses	
	23/7/17		Ambulance sent for sick horse 2/7 Field Ambulance	
	24/7/17		Capt Scott returns from leave Lieut Vaughey evacuated to Base Veterinary Hospital	
	25/7/17		D.A.D.V.S. goes on leave. Cpl Scott takes over duty for him during his absence	
	26/7/17		Cpl Scott inspects horses of 178 Infantry Bde.	

WAR DIARY or INTELLIGENCE SUMMARY

Army Form C. 2118.

Place	Date	Hour	Summary of Events and Information	Remarks and references to Appendices
In the Field	27/7/17		Capt Scrby goes to Amberine to 2/1st N Field Ambulance to see horses. Casing speetted for Parvery. He also Inspects Horses 2/1st Coy R.E.	
	28/7/17		Capt Scrby goes to II Corps Headquarters. General Routine	
	29/7/17		Inspection at 6.30 am by ADVS II Corps. Capt Scrby goes with ADVS II Corps to inspect horses of 167/177 Infantry B & 260 Machine Gun Coy	
	30/7/17		Capt Scrby inspects horses of Sherwood Foresters. Fourteen sick animals evacuated to Base Veterinary Hospital & Capt Scrby goes with 7 S.O.C Section 59 D.A.C. & 176 Field Coy R.E. 175 Machine Gun Coy	
	31/7/17		ADVS II Corps to inspect horses 6/177 Infantry Bde. 176 Field Coy R.E. 175 Machine Gun Coy Capt Scrby inspects horses of II Corps Cyclist Battalion	

Ju G Scrby

WAR DIARY or INTELLIGENCE SUMMARY

Army Form C. 2118

3/1st N. Midl. Veterinary Section
59th N. Div.

Place	Date	Hour	Summary of Events and Information	Remarks and references to Appendices
Pargningig	1/8/17		Capt Sorby doing duties of D.A.D.V.S. 14 animals evacuated to Ross Veterinary Hospital	
"	2/8/17		Capt Sorby vendinghoith horses of 2/1 S.C. attached to 295 Bde Mounted	
"	3/8/17		General Routine. Capt Sorby inspects horses 2/3rd Field Ambulance 59th Div Train Lines	
"	4/8/17		General Routine	
"	5/8/17		7 Animals evacuated to Base Veterinary Hospital. Capt Sorby attends Conference at H.Q 59 Batters	D.V.18 Office
"	6/8/17		Capt Sorby inspects animals of 178 Inf Bde, 470 Field Bry R.E. 175 M.G.C. 75 D.A.C. Section	D.A.C.
"	7/8/17		General Routine	
"	8/8/17		Capt Sorby inspects animals of 200 M.G.C & 469 Field Bry R.E.	
"	9/8/17		" " " 2nd Line Transport 176/177 Infantry Bde	
"	10/8/17		" " " 3/1 Field Ambulance 59" Div Trains & also history of A. H.Q.D.S.	
"	11/8/17		" " " 2nd line Transport 178 Inf Bde	
"	12/8/17		6 Animals evacuated to a Base Veterinary Hospital	
"	13/8/17		S.G Chamber Turret Capt Sorby goes on U.D.W.Q	
"	14/8/17		Capt Sorby meets 178 Inf Bde	
"	15/8/17		General Routine	
"	16/8/17		Back from D.A.D.V.S. 69 Div	
"	17/8/17		Capt Sorby inspects 2/3 F. In field Ambulance	
"	18/8/17		Capt Sorby inspects animals of IV Corps by C.S.N. Batt	
"	19/8/17		Capt Sorby visits sick animals ... Takes over duties of D.A.D.V.S	
"	20/8/17		" " inspects animals of 176/177 Infantry Bdes 174 & 200 M.G Corps 469 & 470 Field Bry. R.E	
"	21/8/17		" " " 3rd Field Ambulance 178 Inf Bde & 3rd Div Train	
"	22/8/17		" " " 469 470 & 467 Field Corps R.E. 2/5 S. Nepth Regt 72/1 Field Ambulance	
Bourguemont	23/8/17		General Routine. Capt Sorby inspects IV Corps Cyclists	
"	24/8/17		General Routine. Cr Bourguemont Covert Union up wounded them	
"	25/8/17		The Unit moves to Bourguemont Covert. Union up wounded them	
"	26/8/17		Capt Sorby inspects animals of 178 Infantry Bde 2nd line, D.A.C. 175 M.G.C. 2/5 S. Nepth Regt.	

WAR DIARY or INTELLIGENCE SUMMARY

Army Form C. 2118.

Place	Date	Hour	Summary of Events and Information	Remarks and references to Appendices
Boyeureul	26/8/17		Capt Scoby inspects animals of 2/5 & 2/6 N. Staff Regts & 6.9 Field Bry R.E.	
	27/8/17		Capt Scoby inspects animals of 178 Infty Bde. No 3 Bay 59th Div received Tomin (Picking up Brent horses)	
	29/8/17		General Routine Capt Scoby inspects animals of 173 Bde.	
	30/8/17		General Routine	
	31/8/17		Unit moves by road to Clocking prior to entraining for Winnezeele	

(Sgd) G Scoby
Capt AVC
O/C

Army Form C. 2118.

WAR DIARY
or
INTELLIGENCE SUMMARY
(Erase heading not required.)

Instructions regarding War Diaries and Intelligence Summaries are contained in F. S. Regs., Part II. and the Staff Manual respectively. Title Pages will be prepared in manuscript.

Place	Date	Hour	Summary of Events and Information	Remarks and references to Appendices
Town	1/9/17		Journey by train from Meteren. Arrive Poperinghe 7 pm. Proceed by road to Vlamertinghe & arrive 11.30 pm	
Vlamertinghe	2/9/17		Billets at a farm on Steenvoorde Road. General duties	
	3/9/17		General Routine. Capt Scoby goes to Div Headquarters	
	4/9/17		General Routine	
	5/9/17		Capt Scoby inspects animals of 2/1st Field Ambulance	
	6/9/17		General Routine	
	7/9/17		4 Horses evacuated by road to 59 MVS. Capt Scoby goes to 178 Bde to inspect animals	
	8/9/17		General Routine	
	9/9/17		Capt Scoby inspects animals of 178 Bde	
	10/9/17		MSW of D.A.D.V.S. 59 Div	
	11/9/17		General Routine	
	12/9/17		Capt Scoby inspects animals of 178 Bde	
	13/9/17		General Routine	
	14/9/17		General Routine. Visit of I.O.A.D. Vet S. 59 Div	
	15/9/17		27 Animals evacuated by road to 59 MVS. Capt Scoby inspects animals of 2/5 & 2/6 Sherwood Foresters	
	16/9/17		Capt Scoby goes to DHQ & 59 Div	
	17/9/17		Capt Scoby inspects animals of 2/7 & 2/8 Sherwood Foresters	
	18/9/17		General Routine	
	19/9/17		34 Animals evacuated by road to 59 MVS	
	20/9/17		Capt Scoby inspects animals of 2/5 & 2/6 Lin Field Ambulance	
	21/9/17		General Routine	
	22/9/17		3 Animals evacuated by road to 59 MVS	
	23/9/17		General Routine	
Vlamertinghe	24/9/17		This MVS proceeds by road to Roundsbrook & takes over from 1/1 East Lancs in U.8.53.6.0	
	25/9/17		Sick Animals evacuated to Base Veterinary Hospital	
	26/9/17		General Routine	
	27/9/17		2 Animals evacuated to Base Veterinary Hospital	Animal remains in existence from returns returned in August
	28/9/17		33 Animals evacuated to Base Veterinary Hospital	
	29/9/17		17 Animals evacuated to Base Veterinary Hospital	
	30/9/17		1 Animal evacuated to Base Veterinary Hospital. General Routine	

WAR DIARY or INTELLIGENCE SUMMARY

Army Form C. 2118.

2/1st N.M. Mobile Veterinary Section 39 Div

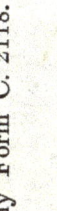

Place	Date	Hour	Summary of Events and Information	Remarks and references to Appendices
Brandhoek	1/10/17		Hand. Camp 7 Sick Animals over to No. 1st New Zealand Mobile Veterinary Section	
Steenbecque	2/10/17		Proceed by road to Steenbecque. 36 Sick Animals evacuated by road to No 23 Veterinary Hospital St Omer.	
"	3/10/17		Inspection of animals of 173 Bde by Capt Scoby	
"	4/10/17		General Routine	
Rupigny	5/10/17		Proceed by road to Rupigny	
"	6/10/17		General Routine	
"	7/10/17		Capt Scoby inspects animals of 173 Bde	
"	8/10/17		General Routine	
"	9/10/17		Horse Management Lecture given to 176 Bde Porkeepers	
"	10/10/17		General Routine	
"	11/10/17		"	
"	12/10/17		Proceed by road to Peuves	
Petit Servins	13/10/17		Proceed by road to Petit Servins. Take over army recently occupied by 1st Canadian Mobile Veterinary Section	
"	14/10/17		Capt Scoby inspects animals of 2/7 Sherwood Foresters	
"	15/10/17		Capt Scoby inspects animals of 2/8 Sherwood Foresters	
"	16/10/17		Capt Scoby inspects animals of 2/8 3/5 Field Ambulance 39 Div	
"	17/10/17		Improvements to Camp. Vacken interior	
"	18/10/17		Capt Scoby inspects remounts at Divl Headquarters. 10 B.I. men arrive from No 5 Veterinary Hospital	
"	19/10/17		Capt Scoby inspects animals of 2/2 & 2/4 Field Ambulance. 10 O.I. men despatched to No 2 Veterinary Hospital	
"	20/10/17		General Routine	
"	21/10/17		Improvements to evacuated Sick animals tomorrow	
"	22/10/17		49 Sick Animals evacuated to No 7 Veterinary Hospital Forges Les Eaux	
"	23/10/17		General Routine	
"	24/10/17		Improvements for evacuation of Sick animals tomorrow	
"	25/10/17		35 Sick Animals evacuated to No 7 Veterinary Hospital Forges Les Eaux	
"	26/10/17		General Routine	
"	27/10/17		"	
"	28/10/17		Proceed by road to Barlin	
Barlin	29/10/17		Two horses joined by Town Major of Mazingarbe — Re Rusty Extinct	
"	30/10/17		General Routine	
"	31/10/17		General Routine	

J. Scoby
Capt AVC I/C

WAR DIARY
or
INTELLIGENCE SUMMARY.
(Erase heading not required.)

Army Form C. 2118.

Instructions regarding War Diaries and Intelligence Summaries are contained in F. S. Regs., Part II. and the Staff Manual respectively. Title pages will be prepared in manuscript.

Vol 10

Place	Date	Hour	Summary of Events and Information	Remarks and references to Appendices
Berles	1/11/17		General Routine. Visit of D.D.V.S. 39 Div	
"	2/11/17		23 Sick animals evacuated to No 7 Base Veterinary Hospital. Forges les Eaux	
"	3/11/17		General Routine. Visit of D.A.D.V.S. 39 Div	
"	4/11/17		Horse removed in Ambulance from Prisoners	
"	5/11/17		Horse removed in Ambulance from Lestigny	
"	6/11/17		32 Sick animals evacuated to No 7 Base Veterinary Hospital Forges les Eaux	
"	7/11/17		General Routine	
"	8/11/17		Horse removed in Ambulance from Petit Servins	
"	9/11/17		33 Sick animals evacuated to No 7 Base Veterinary Hospital Forges les Eaux	
"	10/11/17		General Routine	
"	11/11/17		Horse removed in Ambulance from Lievarey	
"	12/11/17		General Routine. Capt Seeley inspects animals of Fantrain Park Horses	
"	13/11/17		32 G.S. Animals evacuated to No 7 Base Veterinary Hospital Forges les Eaux Rivery	
"	14/11/17		Capt Seeley inspects animals of 11 Canadian Rue School	
"	15/11/17		General Routine	
"	16/11/17		16 Sick animals handed over to 22 Mos. V.S. 1 Sick animal handed over to 1st Cav. Fd. V.S.	

Army Form C. 2118.

WAR DIARY
or
INTELLIGENCE SUMMARY.
(Erase heading not required.)

Instructions regarding War Diaries and Intelligence Summaries are contained in F. S. Regs., Part II. and the Staff Manual respectively. Title pages will be prepared in manuscript.

Place	Date	Hour	Summary of Events and Information	Remarks and references to Appendices
Hannescamp	19/11/17		Moved by march route to Hannescamp	
	20/11/17		General Routine	
	21/11/17		Moved by march route to Bussereux	
Bussereux	22/11/17		General Routine	
"	22/11/17		General Routine	
"	22/11/17		General Routine	
	23/11/17		Moved by route march to Robert C. Petit	
	24/11/17		Moved by march route to Etinencourt	
Bucquoy	25/11/17		General Routine	
"	26/11/17		General Routine	
"	27/11/17		General Routine	
"	28/11/17		6 Animals cast. reported to Corps Veterinary O.O.S.	
"	29/11/17		General Routine	
"	30/11/17		Strength as mustering orders on hand	

G.G. Goss
Captain
M.V.O. No. 59 N. Mid. Vet. Section
59 N. Mid.

Army Form C. 2118.

WAR DIARY
or
INTELLIGENCE SUMMARY.

(Erase heading not required.)

Instructions regarding War Diaries and Intelligence Summaries are contained in F. S. Regs., Part II. and the Staff Manual respectively. Title pages will be prepared in manuscript.

Place	Date	Hour	Summary of Events and Information	Remarks and references to Appendices
Estrineau	1/12/17		General Remarks	
"	2/12/17		Wounded Horses received in Ambulance from Lorries & Glesquieres	
"	3/12/17		Advanced Veterinary Aid Post from ech on Trajet, Trescault Road. Section moves to New received place	
Havrincourt Wood	4/12/17		13 Horses evacuated to Veterinary Casualty Clearing Station	
"	5/12/17		16 Sick animals evacuated to V.C.C.S.	
"	6/12/17		29 Sick & Wounded animals evacuated to Vetry C.C.S.	
"	7/12/17		32 Sick & Wounded animals evacuated to Vetry C.C.S.	
"	8/12/17		19 Sick & Wounded animals evacuated to Vetry C.C.S.	
"	9/12/17		13 Sick & Wounded animals evacuated to Vetry C.C.S.	
"	10/12/17		87 Sick & Wounded animals evacuated to Vetry C.C.S.	
"	11/12/17		20 Sick & Wounded animals evacuated to Vetry C.C.S.	
"	12/12/17		12 Sick & Wounded animals evacuated to Vetry C.C.S.	
"	13/12/17		12 Sick & Wounded animals evacuated to Vetry C.C.S.	
"	14/12/17		5 Sick & Wounded animals evacuated to Vetry C.C.S.	
"	15/12/17		3 Sick & Wounded animals evacuated to Vetry C.C.S.	
"	16/12/17		1 Wounded Mule evacuated to Vetry C.C.S.	

Army Form C. 2118.

WAR DIARY
or
INTELLIGENCE SUMMARY.
(Erase heading not required.)

Instructions regarding War Diaries and Intelligence Summaries are contained in F. S. Regs., Part II. and the Staff Manual respectively. Title pages will be prepared in manuscript.

Place	Date	Hour	Summary of Events and Information	Remarks and references to Appendices
Nanneville	17/12/17		Proceed to Nanneville. A.D.V.S. ? wounded animals evacuated to Vetry C.C.S.	
"	18/12/17		Capt Looby inspects animals of 178 Bde. 7 Sick ? wounded animals evacuated to Vetry C.C.S.	
"	19/12/17		4 animals evacuated to Vetry C.C.S.	
"	20/12/17		25 Sick ? wounded animals evacuated to Vetry C.C.S. Capt Looby inspects animals Royal Irish Rifles	
"	21/12/17		26 Sick ? wounded animals evacuated to Vetry C.C.S.	
"	22/12/17		20 Sick ? wounded animals evacuated to Vetry C.C.S.	
"	23/12/17		10 Sick ? wounded animals evacuated to Vetry C.C.S.	
"	24/12/17		Proceed by route to Achiet le Petit	
"	25/12/17		Proceed by road to La Brayey	
"	26/12/17		General Routine	
"	27/12/17		General Routine	
"	28/12/17		Capt Looby inspects animals of 75 ? 76 Sherwood Foresters	
"	29/12/17		Capt Looby inspects animals of 74 ? 75 Sherwood Foresters	
"	30/12/17		Grey mule collected from Musquicourt our Curcer	
"	31/12/17		General Routine	

WAR DIARY
or
INTELLIGENCE SUMMARY.

(Erase heading not required.)

Army Form C. 2118.

Instructions regarding War Diaries and Intelligence Summaries are contained in F. S. Regs., Part II. and the Staff Manual respectively. Title pages will be prepared in manuscript.

Place	Date	Hour	Summary of Events and Information	Remarks and references to Appendices
Army	1/1/18		Capt Sorley inspected animals of 2/6 N.M. Field Amb. balance of 175 field by R.E. H. Sherwood Foresters, 175 & 6 of by	
"	2/1/18		General Routine	
"	3/1/18		Capt Sorley visits 172 Bde Headquarters & 172 Field by R.E.	
"	4/1/18		Capt Sorley inspects with 2/2 Fd Amb Tracing first line Transport 172 Inf Bde	
"	5/1/18		do 176 Inf Bde	
"	6/1/18		General Routine	
"	7/1/18		12 Sick animals evacuated to Mob. Veterinary Hospital	
"	8/1/18		Capt Sorley inspects with 2/2 Fd Amb Tracing 1st Line Transport 176 Field by R.E. & 2/6 North Staffs	
"	9/1/18		Capt Sorley inspects 2nd Line Transport & 77 Inf Bty	
"	10/1/18		Capt Sorley inspects with G.O.C. animals of 2/6 South Staffs & 2/6 North Staffs Reg ts	
"	11/1/18		General Routine	
"	12/1/18		Capt Sorley visits Bde General of 172 Inf Bde Headquarters	
"	13/1/18		Capt Sorley inspects animals of 2/6 & 2/7 Sherwood Foresters	
"	14/1/18		11 Sick Animals evacuated to No 14 Veterinary Hospital	
"	15/1/18		General Routine	
"	16/1/18		Capt Sorley inspects animals of A/172 Field By R.E. & visits 172 Inf by 72 & Mobile Ambulance, 172 Field By R.E.	

Army Form C. 2118.

WAR DIARY
or
INTELLIGENCE SUMMARY.
(Erase heading not required.)

Instructions regarding War Diaries and Intelligence Summaries are contained in F. S. Regs., Part II. and the Staff Manual respectively. Title pages will be prepared in manuscript.

Place	Date	Hour	Summary of Events and Information	Remarks and references to Appendices
Atwerp	17/1/18		General Routine	
"	18/1/18		Carts Lorry visits 2nd & 3rd R.F.A.	
"	19/1/18		Carts Lorry visits 4.70 Field Bry R.G.	
"	20/1/18		General Routine. 26 Sick animals admitted to Sick Lines	
"	21/1/18		30 Sick animals to No 14 Veterinary Hospital	
"	22/1/18		General Routine. 2 Sick animals admitted to Sick Lines	
"	23/1/18		Eight Sick horses on leave to England. 2 Sick animals admitted to Sick Lines	
"	24/1/18		General Routine. 1 Stray horse admitted to Horse Lines	
"	25/1/18		General Routine	
"	26/1/18		General Routine. 1 Sick Horse admitted	
"	27/1/18		Horse Ambulance from Hyde 177 Infty Bde to Sick Lines of Corpes	
"	28/1/18		12 Animals evacuated to No 14 Veterinary Hospital	
"	29/1/18		General Routine. 2 Sick animals admitted	
"	30/1/18		General Routine	
"	31/1/18		14 Sick Animals admitted to Sick Lines for examination	

W.F.Watson Major A.V.C.
for O/C 2/1 N. Mid Veterinary Section
OVMP

WAR DIARY or INTELLIGENCE SUMMARY

Army Form C. 2118.

No. 4 Mobile Veterinary Section

Place	Date	Hour	Summary of Events and Information	Remarks and references to Appendices
Lebucquiere	1/2/18		17 Sick animals evacuated to No 14 Veterinary Hospital Abbeville	
"	2/2/18		17 Sick animals admitted to Sick lines of Unit. 17 Sick animals evacuated from Bancourt in Ambulance	
"	3/2/18		3 Sick animals admitted to Sick lines, one of which was removed from Bancourt in Ambulance	
"	4/2/18		20 Sick animals evacuated to No 14 Veterinary Hospital Abbeville	
"	5/2/18		General Routine. 3 Sick animals admitted, one of which was fetched in by Ambulance from form at Costinescourt	
"	6/2/18		General Routine	
"	7/2/18		General Routine	
"	8/2/18		Capt Scotty returns from leave to England. 5 Sick animals evacuated to No 14 Veterinary Hospital Abbeville	
"	9/2/18		Proceed by Route March to Ytres	
"	10/2/18		Proceed by Route March to Equillers	
Equillers	11/2/18		12 Sick animals admitted to Sick lines of Unit	
"	12/2/18		6 Sick animals admitted to Sick lines of Unit	
"	13/2/18		Capt Scotty to 176 Infantry Bgd to inspect Transport animals. 3 Sick animals admitted to Sick Lines of Unit	
"	14/2/18		3 Sick animals admitted to Sick Lines of Unit	
"	15/2/18		24 Sick animals evacuated to No 7 Base Veterinary Hospital Argus En lens	
"	16/2/18		General Routine	

Army Form C. 2118.

WAR DIARY
or
INTELLIGENCE SUMMARY.
(Erase heading not required.)

Place	Date	Hour	Summary of Events and Information	Remarks and references to Appendices
Lyellers	17/2/15		General Routine	
"	18/2/15		13 Sick animals admitted to Sick Lines of Unit	
"	19/2/15		15 Sick animals admitted to Sick Lines of Unit	
"	20/2/15		Capt Sorby visits 177 Infantry Bde & 2/2 N.g Company to inspect Transport Animals	
"	21/2/15		13 Sick animals admitted to Sick Lines of Unit	
"	22/2/15		20 Sick animals evacuated to No 1 Base Veterinary Hospital. Horse to Canvas	
"	23/2/15		1 Sick animal destroyed on farm 8/27 Bays Rd in Ambulance	
"	24/2/15		Capt Sorby visits A & B Field Coy R.E. to inspect Transport Animals	
"	25/2/15		20 Sick Animals admitted to Sick Lines of Unit	
"	26/2/15		23 Sick Animals evacuated to No 7 Base Veterinary Hospital	
"	27/2/15		Capt Sorby visits 4 & O Field Coy R.E.	
"	28/2/15		21 Sick Animals admitted to Sick Lines of Unit	

R.J. Sorby Captain
To off c'd in Mobile Veterinary Section

Army Form C. 2118.

WAR DIARY
or
INTELLIGENCE SUMMARY.
(Erase heading not required.)

Instructions regarding War Diaries and Intelligence Summaries are contained in F. S. Regs., Part II. and the Staff Manual respectively. Title pages will be prepared in manuscript.

Place	Date	Hour	Summary of Events and Information	Remarks and references to Appendices
Cuillers	1/3/19		23 Sick Animals evacuated to No 7 Reception Veterinary Hospital Arques les Cenes	
"	2/3/19		General Routine	
"	3/3/19		General Routine	
"	4/3/19		General Routine	
"	5/3/19		Cash Sentry visits 172 Field Bry. 92 & 173 Inf. Bde. 16 neglect Transport Animals	
"	6/3/19		Cash Sentry inspects animals of 9th R.W. Field Ambulance with 16 say for Losses	
"	7/3/19		General Routine	
"	8/3/19		6 Sick animals admitted to Sect Lines for evacuation	
"	9/3/19		General Routine	
"	10/3/19		General Routine	
"	11/3/19		26 Sick animals evacuated to Sect Lines for evacuation	
"	12/3/19		34 Sick animals evacuated to No 7 Reception Veterinary Hospital Arques les Cenes	
"	13/3/19		General Routine	
"	14/3/19		13 Sick animals admitted to Sect Lines for Evacuation	
"	15/3/19		13 Sick animals evacuated to No 7 Reception Veterinary Hospital Arques les Cenes	
"	16/3/19		General Routine	

Army Form C. 2118.

WAR DIARY
or
INTELLIGENCE SUMMARY.
(Erase heading not required.)

Instructions regarding War Diaries and Intelligence Summaries are contained in F. S. Regs., Part II. and the Staff Manual respectively. Title pages will be prepared in manuscript.

51st NORTH MIDLAND MOBILE VETERINARY SECTION

Place	Date	Hour	Summary of Events and Information	Remarks and references to Appendices
Corbehem	17/3/18		General Routine	
"	18/3/18		17 Sck Animals admitted to Sck Lines for evacuation	
"	19/3/18		23 Sck Animals evacuated to No 7 Reut/from Veterinary Hospital Forges les Eaux	
"	20/3/18		Visit of DDVS II Corps	
"	21/3/18	11 am	Proceed to Gonnelieu E route	
Gonnelieu	22/3/18		Proceed by march Route to Ayette	
Ayette	23/3/18		Proceed by march Route to Bayencourt	
Bayencourt	24/3/18		Standing to, awaiting orders	
"	25/3/18		Proceed by march Route to Couin. All Sck Animals evacuated to IV Corps Vetry C.P.S.	
"	26/3/18		Proceed by march Route to Henouville	
Henouville	27/3/18		General Routine	
"	28/3/18		Proceed by march Route to Hunival St Pol	
"	29/3/18		Proceed by march Route to Tangrul	
Tangrul	30/3/18		General Routine	
"	3/3/18		Proceed by march Route to Coyecologne	

R. Shay Captain
2. Officer in Mobile Vety Section

21 2/1st North Highland Mobile Veterinary Section

WAR DIARY
or
INTELLIGENCE SUMMARY

Army Form C. 2118.

(Erase heading not required.)

Place	Date	Hour	Summary of Events and Information	Remarks and references to Appendices
Equicourt	1/4/18		Proceed to Herbergue by Rouen Rente	
Herbergue	2/4/18		Proceed to Preven Road. St Jonston Biezon Road.	
Preven Road	3/4/18		General Routine	
"	4/4/18		Capt Smiley inspects transport & animals of 1/7th Infantry Bde	
"	5/4/18		General Routine	
"	6/4/18		General Routine	
"	7/4/18		Proceed to Broadheck 3 Sick Animals admitted	
Broadheck	8/4/18		6 Animals admitted to Sick Lines	
"	9/4/18	10 a.m	9 Animals evacuated to Sick Lines Blacksmith 1st S.B. Kroner wounded by Enemy Shellfire not wounded sufficient	
"	9/4/18	2 p.m	10 Animals evacuated to 7th Corps V.C.S.	
"	10/4/18		9 Animals admitted to Sick Lines 9 animals evacuated to 7th Corps V.C.S.	
"	11/4/18		8 Animals admitted to Sick Lines 7 animals evacuated to 7th Corps V.C.S.	
"	12/4/18		9 Animals admitted to Sick Lines 8 animals evacuated to 7th Corps V.C.S.	
"	13/4/18		Proceed to Rbli.	
Albert	10/4/18		General Routine	
"	13/4/18		5 Animals admitted to Sick Lines	

Army Form C. 2118.

WAR DIARY
or
INTELLIGENCE SUMMARY.
(Erase heading not required.)

Instructions regarding War Diaries and Intelligence Summaries are contained in F. S. Regs., Part II. and the Staff Manual respectively. Title pages will be prepared in manuscript.

Place	Date	Hour	Summary of Events and Information	Remarks and references to Appendices
Abuli	16/4/18		General Routine	
Abuli	17/4/18		7 Animals evacuated to Sick Lines	
"	18/4/18		13 Animals evacuated to 22 A/p V.F.S	
"	19/4/18		Proceed to St Sixte	
St Sixte	20/4/18		General Routine	
"	21/4/18		Proceed to Bumbeque	
Bumbeque	22/4/18		General Routine	
"	23/4/18		Animals evacuated to Sick Lines	
"	24/4/18		10 Animals evacuated to No 1 V.G.S.	
"	25/4/18		General Routine	
"	26/4/18		"	
"	27/4/18		7 Animals evacuated to Sick Lines. 6 animals evacuated	
"	28/4/18		General Routine	
"	29/4/18		General Routine	
"	30/4/18		General Routine	

Army Form C. 2118.

2/H.H. Mobile Veterinary Section

WAR DIARY
or
INTELLIGENCE SUMMARY.
(Erase heading not required.)

Nov 16

Place	Date	Hour	Summary of Events and Information	Remarks and references to Appendices
BAMBECQUE	1/5/18		General Routine	
"	2/5/18		General Routine	
"	3/5/18		General Routine	
"	4/5/18		Proceed &c	
"	5/5/18		General Routine	
"	6/5/18		General Routine	
"	7/5/18		Proceed to Leggers Cappel by route march	
"	8/5/18		Proceed to St Omer by route march	
"	9/5/18		Proceed to Hammerby by route march	
"	10/5/18		Proceed to Precy Eg Ponces by route march	
"	11/5/18		General Routine	
"	12/5/18		Proceed to Eps by route march	
EPS	13/5/18		2 Sick Horses admitted to sick lines. 1 Animal returned to Unit Church	
"	14/5/18		General Routine	
"	15/5/18		3 Sick Animals admitted to Sick Lines	
"	16/5/18		General Routine	

WAR DIARY or INTELLIGENCE SUMMARY.

Army Form C. 2118.

(Erase heading not required.)

Place	Date	Hour	Summary of Events and Information	Remarks and references to Appendices
DIEVAL	17/5/18		Proceed to DIEVAL	
"	18/5/18		2 Sick animals admitted to Sick Lines	
"	19/5/18		6 Sick animals admitted to Sick Lines. 1 Animal returned to Unit owner.	
"	20/5/18		11 Sick animals evacuated to No 1 Veterinary Evacuation Station, BARLIN	
"	21/5/18		1 Sick animal admitted. Capt Sodymichaels animals of No Northumberland Fusiliers & 11 Royal Berkshires	
"	22/5/18		4 Sick animals admitted to Sick Lines	
"	23/5/18		2 Sick animals admitted to Sick Lines	
"	24/5/18		7 Sick animals evacuated to No 1 Veterinary Evacuation their Station BARLIN. 1 Sick animal admitted	
"	25/5/18		General Routine	
"	26/5/18		General Routine	
"	27/5/18		3 Sick animals admitted to Sick Lines	
"	28/5/18		4 Sick animals admitted to Sick Lines	
"	29/5/18		6 Sick animals evacuated to Canadian Corps Veterinary Evacuation Station, OURTON	
"	30/5/18		1 Sick animal admitted to Sick Lines	
"	31/5/18		General Routine	

Ruof Bost Capt AVC

Army Form C. 2118.

WAR DIARY
or
INTELLIGENCE SUMMARY.
(Erase heading not required.)

11 21st D.A.C. Vet: Offr Section
     59th Divn

Vol 17

Instructions regarding War Diaries and Intelligence Summaries are contained in F. S. Regs., Part II. and the Staff Manual respectively. Title pages will be prepared in manuscript.

Place	Date	Hour	Summary of Events and Information	Remarks and references to Appendices
In the field	1/6/18		Sergt Smith, Smith, granted leave to England from 1/6/18 to 15/6/18. Lionel Roulin	
"	2/6/18		Lionel Roulin	
"	3/6/18		2 animals admitted to sick lines. Lionel Roulin	
"	4/6/18		3 animals evacuated to X Corps O.E.S. Pt: Wty: picquets on lines. Lionel Roulin	
"	5/6/18		Lionel Roulin	
"	6/6/18		Capt: foot patrols on lines. Lionel Roulin	
"	7/6/18		1046 P/a/ Lieut Ellison, E. posted to 2 Vety Hospital. Lionel Roulin	
"	8/6/18		Lionel Roulin	
"	9/6/18		Lionel Roulin	at sick lines
"	10/6/18		Capt. Vety: Inspect: animals at 2/3 Field Ambulance, 1st Hy-Cy R.G.A. & 11th Royal Scots. animals admitted	
"	11/6/18		Capt: Vety: patrols to lines. 1 animal admitted to sick lines. Lionel Roulin	
"	12/6/18		Capt: Vety: inspect: animals at 467 Field Co R.E. animals evacuated K.S.Corps O.E.S. Lionel Roulin	
"	13/6/18		Capt: Vety: patrols to lines. Lionel Roulin	
"	14/6/18		Capt: Vety: inspect: animals at Royal East Kent Yeoms. & 9 Northumberland Fusiliers. Lionel Roulin	
"	15/6/18		Lionel Roulin	
"	16/6/18		2 animals admitted to sick lines. Lionel Roulin	

Army Form C. 2118.

WAR DIARY
or
INTELLIGENCE SUMMARY.
(Erase heading not required.)

2/1 Y.Y. Mythil Vety Section

Place	Date	Hour	Summary of Events and Information	Remarks and references to Appendices
In the Field	17/6/18		2 animals evacuated to X Cav. C.C.S. General Routine	
"	18/6/18		Section gone to Romy. The Smith returns from leave. Capt. Toby takes over D.N.Q. duties	
"	19/6/18		Capt. Toby visits units at Romy and to our Lawn & Liskey. General Routine	
"	20/6/18		3 horses admitted to sick lines. Capt. Toby visits 2/1 Field Ambulance	
"	21/6/18		General Routine. Visits units at Lawn & Liskey	
"	22/6/18		Capt. Toby inspects Royal Welsh Fusiliers Regt. at Romy. General Routine	
"	23/6/18		Inspects animals of No. 2 D.N.Q.	
"	24/6/18		1 animal admitted to sick lines. Capt. Toby visits units. General Routine	
"	25/6/18		3 animals admitted to sick lines	
"	26/6/18		5 animals evacuated to X Capt. C.C.S.	
"	27/6/18		3 animals admitted to sick lines. General Routine	
"	28/6/18		Capt. Toby visits No. 2 Coy. A.S.C. General Routine	
"	29/6/18		1 animal admitted to sick lines. Capt. Toby visits No. 2 D.N.Q. Coy. 2 D.N.Q.	
"	30/6/18		1 animal admitted to sick lines. General Routine	

Guy Toby O'Hara

Army Form C. 2118.

WAR DIARY
or
INTELLIGENCE SUMMARY.
(Erase heading not required.)

Instructions regarding War Diaries and Intelligence Summaries are contained in F. S. Regs., Part II. and the Staff Manual respectively. Title pages will be prepared in manuscript.

*2/1st NORTH MIDLAND MOBILE VETERINARY SECTION * JUL 1918*

Vol 1

Place	Date	Hour	Summary of Events and Information	Remarks and references to Appendices
Bovry	1/7/18		3 Animals evacuated to I Vety Evacuation Station. 1 Sick animal admitted. 1st Sub Sec of Bapaume	
do	2/7/18		General Routine	
do	3/7/18		General Routine	
do	4/7/18		2 Sick Animals admitted	
do	5/7/18		1 Sick Animal admitted	
do	6/7/18		General Routine	
do	7/7/18		General Routine	
do	8/7/18		5 Sick Animals admitted	
do	9/7/18		6 Sick Animals evacuated to I Veterinary Evacuation Station	
do	10/7/18		General Routine	
do	11/7/18		Proceed by Route march to Tincourt Cappeur	
Tincourt Cappeur	12/7/18		Capt Bousby inspects animals 17th Infantry Bde & 2/1st N Field Ambulance	
	13/7/18		3 Sick Animals admitted	
	14/7/18		General Routine	
	15/7/18		Captain Lee inspects animals of 27th Coy R.O.C. & 7/1st N Field Ambulance	
	16/7/18		General Routine	

Army Form C. 2118.

WAR DIARY
or
INTELLIGENCE SUMMARY.
(Erase heading not required.)

Instructions regarding War Diaries and Intelligence Summaries are contained in F. S. Regs., Part II. and the Staff Manual respectively. Title pages will be prepared in manuscript.

21st NORTH MIDLAND MOBILE VETERINARY SECTION — JUL 1918

Place	Date	Hour	Summary of Events and Information	Remarks and references to Appendices
Arrived Rosieux	1/7/18		Capt Sorby inspects animals of 17th Infantry Bde with A.D.V.S. 59th Divn, 3 Sick animals admitted	
do	6/7/18		General Routine	
do	18/7/18		A.D.V.S. visits the Section	
do	20/7/17		6 Sick animals evacuated to No 2 Veterinary Collecting Post. Capt Sorby inspects animals of 23rd Field Ambulance	
do	21/7/18		General Routine	
do	22/7/18		Capt Sorby inspects animals of 23rd Kings Liverpool Regt. Six of these removed in Ambulance from the lines evacuated to No 1 Veterinary Collecting Post	
do	23/7/18		2 Sick animals evacuated to No 1 Veterinary Collecting Post	
do	24/7/18		General Routine	
do	25/7/18		General Routine	
"	26/7/18		Arrived Maricourt by Congue to Bossieux	
Bossieux	27/7/18		Capt Sorby inspects animals of 470 Bty R.G.A. 1 S.A.A. Field Ambulance 5 Sick animals admitted, 2 evacuated	
"	28/7/18		7 Sick animals admitted. 3 Sick animals evacuated to No 1 Veterinary Evacuation Station	
"	29/7/17		15 Sick animals admitted. Capt Sorby inspects animals of 23rd Divn M.G.C.	
"	30/7/17		21 Sick animals evacuated. 7 Sick animals admitted. Capt Sorby visits 23rd Divn M.G.C.	
"	31/7/18		11 Sick animals admitted. Capt Sorby inspects animals of 167-170 Field Cos R.E.	

Any Sorby
Capt R.A.V.C

Army Form C. 2118.

WAR DIARY
or
INTELLIGENCE SUMMARY.
(Erase heading not required.)

Place	Date	Hour	Summary of Events and Information	Remarks and references to Appendices
BASSEUX	1/5/10		11 Sick animals evacuated to No 6 b/to M.C.S. 7 Sick Animals evacuated to Sick Lines	
"	2/5/17		Capt Sargapiets animals of 25 Bn Machine Gun Corps. 2 Sick Animals admitted to Sick Lines	
"	3/5/13		2 Sick Animals admitted to Sick Lines. 11 Sick Animals evacuated to No 6 M.C.S.	
"	4/5/13		Received 1 recovered from WALLY in Horse Ambulance	
"	5/5/10		2 Sick Animals admitted to Sick Lines	
"	6/5/13		2 Sick Animals admitted to Sick Lines 6 Sick Animals evacuated to No 6 M.C.S.	
"	7/5/13		4 Sick Animals evacuated	
"	8/5/10		5 Sick Animals admitted. 8 Sick Animals evacuated to No 6 M.C.S. Capt Sorby inspects animals of 176 Inf Bde	
"	9/5/10		6 Sick Animals admitted	
"	10/5/13		2 Sick Animals admitted 5 Sick animals evacuated to No 6 M.C.S	
"	11/5/13		2 Sick Animals admitted	
"	12/5/13		2 Sick Animals admitted 3 Sick Animals evacuated to No 6 M.C.S.	
"	13/5/13		3 Sick Animals admitted. 4 Sick Animals evacuated to No 6 M.C.S.	
"	14/5/13		4 Sick Animals admitted. Capt Sorby inspects animals of 176 Inf Bde	
"	15/5/13		4 Sick Animals admitted 9 Sick Animals evacuated to No 6 M.C.S. Capt Sorby inspects animals of 228 Bde M.G.C.	
"	1/5/13		9 Sick Animals admitted	

Army Form C. 2118.

WAR DIARY
or
INTELLIGENCE SUMMARY.
(Erase heading not required.)

Instructions regarding War Diaries and Intelligence Summaries are contained in F. S. Regs., Part II. and the Staff Manual respectively. Title pages will be prepared in manuscript.

Place	Date	Hour	Summary of Events and Information	Remarks and references to Appendices
BASSEUX	17/5/18		2 Sick Animals admitted. 10 Sick Animals evacuated to No 6 V.E.S.	
"	18/5/18		1 Sick Animal admitted. Capt Sooty inspects animals of A.S.C. Field Coy. R.E.	
"	19/5/18		3 Sick Animals evacuated to No 6 V.E.S. 3 Sick Animals admitted. Capt Sooty inspects animals of 173 & 172 Field Coy	
"	20/5/18		5 Sick Animals admitted. 11 Sick Animals evacuated to No 6 V.E.S.	
"	21/5/18		1 Sick Animal admitted.	
"	22/5/18		21 Sick Animals Admitted with Sick Lines. 9 Sick Animals evacuated to No 6 V.E.S.	
"	23/5/18		21 Sick Animals Evacuated to No 6 V.E.S	
"	23/5/18 10.30am		Proceed by route march to RE-BREUVIETTE	
"	20/5/18 4.30 pm		Proceed by route march to MONCHY CAYEUX	
"	25/5/18		Proceed by route march to NORRENT FONTES	
NORRENT FONTES	26/5/18		General Routine	
"	27/5/18		General Routine	
"	28/5/18		Proceed to TREIZENNES	
TREIZENNES	29/5/18		General Routine. 2 Sick Animals admitted	
"	30/5/18		General Routine	
"	31/5/18		2 Sick Animals Evacuated. Proceed to GUARBECQUE	

Guy J Cook
to 4th/5th Army Vety Service

17

2/5th North Midland Mobile Veterinary Section

WAR DIARY
or
INTELLIGENCE SUMMARY

Army Form C. 2118.

(Erase heading not required.)

Place	Date	Hour	Summary of Events and Information	Remarks and references to Appendices
GUARBEGUE	1/9/18		14 Sick Animals admitted to Sick Lines	
do	2/9/18		16 Sick Animals evacuated to No 11 Veterinary Evacuating Station. 3 Sick Animals admitted to Sick Lines	
do	3/9/18		6 Sick Animals evacuated to No 11 Veterinary Evacuating Station. 3 Sick Animals admitted to Sick Lines	
do	4/9/18		General Routine	
do	5/9/18		7 Sick Animals admitted to Sick Lines. 2 Sick animals evacuated to No 1 Veterinary Evacuating Station	
do	6/9/18 10 a.m.		20 Sick Animals admitted to Sick Lines	
do	6/9/18 12 noon		25 Sick Animals evacuated to No 11 V.E.S.	
do	6/9/18 10.30 pm		Moved to G.H.Q. a 6.0. HAYSTACK FARM	
HAYSTACK FARM	7/9/18		6 Sick Animals admitted to Sick Lines	
do	8/9/18		7 Sick Animals evacuated to No 11 V.E.S. Capt Scarlet R. proceeds on leave to United Kingdom	
do	9/9/18		Command of Unit taken over by Major Bright D.A.D.V.S. 39 Div	
do	10/9/18		5 Sick animals admitted. 1 Sick animal evacuated to No 11 V.E.S.	
do	11/9/18		4 Sick Animals admitted. 1 Sick Animal evacuated to No 11 V.E.S.	
do	12/9/18		Quantity of Salvage collected and this Unit returned to Salvage Dump	
do	13/9/18		3 Sick Animals admitted. 1 Sick animal evacuated to No 11 V.E.S. 1 Bad Horse removed from AIRE on to Lines	
do	14/9/18		8 Sick Animals admitted to Sick Lines	

Army Form C. 2118.

2/1/1/1 North Midland Veterinary Section

WAR DIARY
or
INTELLIGENCE SUMMARY.

(Erase heading not required.)

Instructions regarding War Diaries and Intelligence Summaries are contained in F. S. Regs., Part II. and the Staff Manual respectively. Title pages will be prepared in manuscript.

Place	Date	Hour	Summary of Events and Information	Remarks and references to Appendices
71st A.V.C. Shed 36A HAYSTACK FARM	15/9/17		5 Sick & Wounded animals evacuated to No 11 V.C.S. 7 Sick animals admitted to Sick Lines	
do	16/9/17		5 Sick & Wounded animals admitted to Sick Lines. 6 Sick animals evacuated to No 11 V.C.S.	
do	17/9/17		7 Sick animals admitted to Sick Lines	
do	18/9/17		7 Sick animals evacuated to No 11 V.C.S. Animal ambulance one (1) wait returned to this command from REIZ. BAILLEUL. Div A.S.C. Supply Col.	Wounded horse remained for ambulance
do	19/9/17		4 Sick animals admitted to Sick Lines	
do	20/9/17		3 Sick animals evacuated to No 11 V.C.S.	
do	21/9/17		2 Sick animals admitted to Sick Lines	
do	22/9/17		1 Sick animal admitted to Sick Lines. One animal admitted Section 7 August returned to this Col. animal	
do	23/9/17		12 Sick & Wounded animals evacuated to No 11 V.C.S.	
do	24/9/17		1 Sick animal admitted to Sick Lines	
do	25/9/17		1 Sick animal admitted to Sick Lines. One remount collecting post formed at LLISTREM R14309 Div.A.S.A	
do	26/9/17		3 Sick animals evacuated to No 11 V.C.S. Capt Sealy Le returns from leave and assumes cmd of Unit	
do	27/9/17		2 Sick animals admitted for subsequent removal by Div Loans with A.P.V.S A Cavpts 2/Lt Lynn	
do	28/9/17		1 Sick animal admitted. 5 Sick animals evacuated to No 11 V.C.S. L/cpl R.W. Bissing Nell 252	
do	29/9/17		2 Sick & Wounded animals admitted	
do	30/9/17		1 Sick Wounded animal commission to No 11 V.C.S.	

R. P. Sealy

To Major in Field Veterinary Veterinary Section

2/1st N.M. MOBILE VETERINARY SECTION.

WAR DIARY
or
INTELLIGENCE SUMMARY.

Army Form C. 2118.

Vol 2

Place	Date	Hour	Summary of Events and Information	Remarks and references to Appendices
G.19.c.6.0 Sht.36A HAYSTACK FARM	1/10/18		General Routine	
do	2/10/18		5 Wounded animals evacuated to Sick Lines	
do	3/10/18		5 Wounded animals evacuated to No 11 V.E.S.	
ESTAIRS – Sht.36A NEUF/BERQUIN RD	4/10/18		Proceed to L.22.C.2.3 Sheet 36A Estairs – Neuf Berquin Road. 5 Sick animals evacuated to No 11 V.E.S. Capt Sorley inspects animals of 175 Inf Bde.	
do	6/10/18		4 Sick animals evacuated to No 11 V.E.S.	
do	7/10/18		4 Sick wounded animals admitted to Sick Lines	
do	8/10/18		3 Sick animals returned to Sick Lines	
do	9/10/18		4 Sick animals admitted to Sick Lines	
do	9/10/18		9 Sick animals evacuated to No 11 V.E.S.	
do	10/10/18		1 Sick animal admitted to Sick Lines. Unit proceeds to G.17 Central Sht 36	
G.17 CENTRAL SHEET 36	11/10/18		2 Sick animals evacuated to No 11 V.E.S. Capt Sorley inspects animals of 176 Inf Bde.	
do	12/10/18			
do	13/10/18		3 Sick animals transferred sent to No 11 V.E.S.	
do	14/10/18		4 Sick animals admitted to Sick Lines	
do	15/10/18		4 Sick animals evacuated to No 11 V.E.S.	
do	16/10/18		2 Sick animal admitted to Sick lines. Capt Sorley inspects animals of 176 Inf Bde Bgt. Group	

2/1 North Midland Mobile Veterinary Section.

Army Form C. 2118.

WAR DIARY
or
INTELLIGENCE SUMMARY.
(Erase heading not required.)

Instructions regarding War Diaries and Intelligence Summaries are contained in F. S. Regs., Part II. and the Staff Manual respectively. Title pages will be prepared in manuscript.

2/1ST NORTH MIDLAND * MOBILE VETERINARY SECTION *
OCT. 1918

Place	Date	Hour	Summary of Events and Information	Remarks and references to Appendices
G.17 CENTRAL SHEET 36	1/10/18		4 Sick animals admitted to sick lines	
do	15/10/18		3 Sick animals evacuated to 11 V.E.S.	
do	17/10/18		Unit proceeds to St Andre K20 c 9.8 Sheet 36. 8 Sick animals collected for evacuation to sick lines	
do	18/10/18		Unit proceeds to HEM G20 C5.3 Sheet 57. No billeting post found at ST ANDRE to which all sick	
G.20. C 5.3. S.57	19/10/18		horses and 11 to sent until the H.Q.S can move forward	
do	21/10/18		3 Sick animals admitted & sent to ST. ANDRE	
do	22/10/18		10 Sick animals admitted	
do	23/10/18		6 Sick animals sent to the collecting post at ST ANDRE	
do	25/10/18		Capt Sortey evacuated animals of 46 Inf Bde	
do	24/10/18		2 Sick animals admitted to sick lines	
do	25/10/18		No 11 V.E.S arrives at La MADELAINE 27 Sick animals evacuated Total 11 V.E.S. Madelaine Withdrawn	
do	30/10/18		5 Sick animals admitted to sick lines	
do	27/10/18		3 Sick animals admitted to sick lines	
do	28/10/18		2 Sick animals transferred sick to No 11 V.E.S	
do	29/10/18		2 Sick animals admitted 5 Sick animals transferred sick to No 11 V.E.S	
do	30/10/18		Capt Sortey evacuated animals of King Edwards Horse	
do	31/10/18			To 31/10/18 to host Vetry Services

WAR DIARY or INTELLIGENCE SUMMARY.

(Erase heading not required.) Army Form C. 2118.

Place	Date	Hour	Summary of Events and Information	Remarks and references to Appendices
G20 65~3 SHEET 37 HEM	1/11/18		7 Sick & Wounded Animals evacuated to Sick Lines	
do	2/11/18		7 Sick Animals evacuated to 11 V.C.S. 4 Sick Animal Remounts evacuated to Sick Lines	
do	3/11/18		Capt Sorley inspects animals of 176 Inf. Bde.	
do	4/11/18		Capt Sorley inspects animals of 2/3~Sterlings Royal Rifles. 5 Sick Animals evacuated to No 11 V.C.S.	
do	5/11/18		3 Sick Animals admitted to Sick Lines	
do	6/11/18		Capt Sorley inspects animals of 176 Inf. Bde & 2/4th N. Field Ambulance. 3 Sick animals admitted	
do	7/11/18		General Routine	
do	8/11/18		4 Wounded Horses evacuated. 92 Horses evacuated. Capt Sorley inspects animals of 2~ Bn K.R.R.	
do	9/11/18		4 Horses evacuated to No 11 V.C.S.	
do	10/11/18		Proceed to BAILLEUL H17 D 8.2 Sheet 37.	
SHEET 37 BAILLEUL	11/11/18		General Routine	
do	12/11/18		Capt Sorley inspects animals of 1/7th & 8th Sussex Regts & 2/5th 4th Field Ambulance. 3 Sick & Wounded animals admitted	
do	13/11/18		2 Animals Evacuated. Sect 70 to 11 V.C.S.	
do	14/11/18		Capt Sorley visits 176 Field Coy R.E. & inspects animals	
do	15/11/18		Proceed by French Route to TRESSIN M20 a1~7 Sheet 37.	
do	16/11/18		Proceed by French route to SECLIN V.29 c.9.3. Sheet 36.	

Army Form C. 2118.

2/3rd N.M. MOBILE VETERINARY SECTION.

WAR DIARY or INTELLIGENCE SUMMARY.
(Erase heading not required.)

Instructions regarding War Diaries and Intelligence Summaries are contained in F.S. Regs., Part II. and the Staff Manual respectively. Title pages will be prepared in manuscript.

Place	Date	Hour	Summary of Events and Information	Remarks and references to Appendices
Vag 6 g.5" Sheet 36 SEGLIN	17/11/18		General Routine	
do	18/11/18		5 Sick Animals admitted to Sick Lines	
do	19/11/18		Visit of A.D.V.S. XI Corps & DDVS N.S. 59th Dn	
do	20/11/18		General Routine	
do	21/11/18		5 Sick animals transferred sick to No 11 V.C.S. 7 Sick animals admitted	
do	22/11/18		6 Sick animals evacuated to No 11 V.C.S	
do	23/11/18		General Routine	
do	24/11/18		3 Sick Animals admitted to Sick Lines	
do	25/11/18		Capt Sorby inspects animals of 1/7th Inf Bde. 5 Sick Animals admitted to Sick Lines	
do	26/11/18		3 Sick Animals evacuated to No 11 V.C.S	
do	27/11/18		General Routine	
do	28/11/18		3 Sick Animals admitted to Sick Lines. Capt Sorby inspects animals of 2/3rd bn King's Royal Rifle Corps	
do	29/11/18		2 Sick animals admitted to Sick Lines	
do	30/11/18		General Routine	

J E Sorby
Capt AVC
O/C 2/3 N.M. Mobile Veterinary Section

2/1st N. Midland Mobile Veterinary Section

Army Form C. 2118.

WAR DIARY
or
INTELLIGENCE SUMMARY.
(Erase heading not required.)

Instructions regarding War Diaries and Intelligence Summaries are contained in F. S. Regs., Part II. and the Staff Manual respectively. Title pages will be prepared in manuscript.

[Stamp: 2/1st NORTH MIDLAND MOBILE VETERINARY SECTION 31 DEC 1918]

Place	Date	Hour	Summary of Events and Information	Remarks and references to Appendices
Loken	1/12/18		Held sick inspection parade of 2/6th Royal North Staffords at H.Q. Left sick Horses admitted. General Routine.	
"	2/12/18		Visit sick inspection parade at 176th Inf. Brigade. 2 Left sick dog to 2. General Routine.	
"	3/12/18		Capt. Roberts visits D.H.Q. Holds postmortem on animal belonging to 2nd Bn. Sea. Rif.	
"	4/12/18		Capt. Roberts inspects animals of 2/1st Field Ambulance. Inspection of Y.D.C.	
"	5/12/18		Moved to Paslti. K.33 a 52 Sheet B.41.	
Paslti	7/12/18		Tidying up of Camp. Capt. Roberts visits 11th P.R.G. Pt. Cavalry Division	
"	8/12/18		Reinit Camp. Capt. Roberts inspects animals belonging to Royal North Staffs. General Poultry	
"	9/12/18		Hold Sick Parade S.A.D.V.S. inspects animals of 176th Inf. Bde. General Poultry	
"	10/12/18		Capt. Roberts takes one Mule to 59 M.V.S. Inspects animals of 2/1st Field Amb. H.Q.R.	
"	11/12/18		Duties of Section Routine. General Poultry	
"	12/12/18		Inspects Animals at D.H.Q. of 10 & Horses 1/1 H.T. General collected.	
"	13/12/18		Inspects Animals at 1st Cav. A. Regt. R.E. General Routine.	
"	14/12/18		Inspects Animals of 2/1 R.J.A. 10 at sick at 5.10 Poultry Comments examined. One & Horses	
"	15/12/18		Inspects Animals of Royal North Staffs. 9 animals admitted 4 to H.Q.V.D.	
"	16/12/18		Visits D.H.Q. & family of General Inch. Cake examined. General Routine.	
"	17/12/18		Inspects animals at 2/1 Field Amb. 15 animals evacuated. Ambulance collected animals for no. 2 Section 59 V.D.	

WAR DIARY
or
INTELLIGENCE SUMMARY.

(Erase heading not required.)

Army Form C. 2118.

Place	Date	Hour	Summary of Events and Information	Remarks and references to Appendices
Berlin	1/12/18		Capt. Lochy attends parade for selection of 2nd grade at Berlin. gone to horse of Hussar Guard Pavilion	
	5/12/18		" " attends parade of Hussar Guards. Also Herr Major de Geradin's Cavalry. 1 admitted	
	8/12/18		Capt. Lochy evacuates animals at 95 K.R.P.R.S. Evac. Hospital. 13 animals admitted.	
	9/12/18		Capt. Lochy evacuates L.H.Q. Hammels admitted	
	11/12/18		Cavalry at 7 p.m. 16 animals called 1 animal from officer R.H.A. wounded cast animal	
	18/12/18		Capt. Lochy inspects animals of Royal Welsh Fusiliers made hay supply to Lithuania bread supplies	
	19/12/18		Visits Sir Carlton horse attachments in horse Guards Place admitted.	
	22/12/18		Capt. Lochy visits Field Cavalry at Arrow. Inspect animals at C.P. Field Ambulance Lahore.	
	23/12/18		Capt. Lochy 17th Hus. Hd. Qts. Renewed D.D.V.S. office to Braren Kaserne.	
	25/12/18		Capt. Lochy inspects animals at Gueb in dist. of horses of 18th Hus. at Lerin. Picton animal admitted.	
	27/12/18		Capt. Lochy inspects animals at 207 Field Cpt. R.E. 16 animals admitted. Evac Kaserne.	
	28/12/18		Rcd. C.R. Cpl. Cpl. York. Berth	
	29/12/18		Capt. Lochy attends horse of C.F. C.R. clas in respect of all animals.	
	30/12/18		Capt. Lochy attends horse of L.H.B. for classify making of all animals 16 horses evacuated	
	31/12/18		Capt. Lochy attends horse at D.H.Q. classify making of all animals 22 horses admitted.	

Ruy Borten Capt.

WAR DIARY
or
INTELLIGENCE SUMMARY.
(Erase heading not required.)

Army Form C. 2118.

Instructions regarding War Diaries and Intelligence Summaries are contained in F. S. Regs., Part II. and the Staff Manual respectively. Title pages will be prepared in manuscript.

Place	Date	Hour	Summary of Events and Information	Remarks and references to Appendices
Borden	1/1/19		General Routine. 12 horses admitted to Sick Lines	
"	2/1/19		Capt Scotty attends Veterinary Board at A.S.C. Sch. R.P.C. 18 Sick animals evacuated to RB30th VES	
"	3/1/19		General Routine. 4 Sick animals admitted to Sick lines	
"	4/1/19		Capt Scotty attends Veterinary Board at A.S.C. Bath Z.B.R.A. 4 Sick animals admitted	
"	5/1/19		" General Routine	
"	6/1/19		General Routine. 5 Sick animals admitted & 14 evacuated to N°30th VES	
"	7/1/19		Capt Scotty attends Veterinary Board at A.S.C. Sch R.P.C. General Routine	
"	8/1/19		" 4 Sick animals admitted	
"	9/1/19		" General Routine. 3 Sick animals admitted	
"	10/1/19		General Routine. 19 Sick animals evacuated to N°30 Corps V.S.S.	
"	11/1/19		General Routine	
"	12/1/19		Capt Scotty walking Horses of Lectors. General Routine	
"	13/1/19		" 25 Bn Kings Liverpool 5 Sick animals admitted & 6 evacuated to N°30 Corps V.E.S.	
"	14/1/19		General Routine. 6 Sick animals evacuated to N°30 Corps V.E.S.	
"	15/1/19		" Capt Scotty inspects horses of 25 Bn Kings Liverpool	
"	16/1/19		" 25 Bn Kings Royal Rifles & 25 y Dragoons for revision	

3914 2/1 NM Feb 16/7 Army Form C. 2118.

WAR DIARY
or
INTELLIGENCE SUMMARY.
(Erase heading not required.)

Vol 2

Place	Date	Hour	Summary of Events and Information	Remarks and references to Appendices
Berlin	1/1/19		General Routine 12 horses admitted to sick lines	
"	2/1/19		Capt Sorby attended Veterinary Parade of 19 & Bde R.F.a. 18 sick horses evacuated to 17 V.C.S.	
"	3/1/19		General Routine 4 sick animals admitted to sick lines	
"	4/1/19		Capt Sorby attended Veterinary Parade of 295 Bde R.F.a. 4 sick animals admitted to sick lines	
"	5/1/19		General Routine	
"	6/1/19		General Routine 5 horses admitted & 14 sick animals evacuated to XV Corps V.C.S.	
"	7/1/19		General Routine Capt Sorby attended Veterinary Parade at 295 Bde R.F.a.	
"	8/1/19		" " " " 4 sick animals admitted	
"	9/1/19		" " General Routine	
"	10/1/19		5 horses admitted	
"	11/1/19		General Routine 16 animals evacuated to XV Corps V.C.S.	
"	12/1/19		General Routine	
"	13/1/19		Capt Sorby Mallein Horses of Colon General Remfrey	
"	14/1/19		" Mallein horses of 295 Bde Kings Liverpool 6 horses evacuated & admitted to sick lines	
"	15/1/19		General Routine 6 sick animals evacuated to XV Corps V.C.S.	
"	16/1/19		Capt Sorby mallein horses of 1/5 Bn Kings Royal Rifles	
"			" " " B5 Bn Kings Royal Rifles 23 horses of horses	

WAR DIARY
or
INTELLIGENCE SUMMARY.
(Erase heading not required.)

Army Form C. 2118.

Instructions regarding War Diaries and Intelligence Summaries are contained in F. S. Regs., Part II. and the Staff Manual respectively. Title pages will be prepared in manuscript.

Place	Date	Hour	Summary of Events and Information	Remarks and references to Appendices
Berlin	14/4/19		Capt Scotty admitted to Ossnonry Hosfil. 2 L/Sj 27 Bn. A.I.F. & 2Cpl. arrivals as invalid to U.K.	
"	18/4/19		" " " " General Routine	
"	19/4/19		" " " " 4 arrivals admitted to Sick line	
"	20/4/19		" Yestde XI Corps Field Cashier. General Routine	
"	21/4/19		General Routine. 6 Sick arrivals evacuated to XI Corps T.Hos.	
"	22/4/19		General Routine	
"	23/4/19		Capt Scotty visits 25 Brit R.R. for Meallowing of officers Messes	
"	24/4/19		Capt Scotty proceeds on leave to U.K. Capt Rupier takes over General Routine	
"	25/4/19		Capt Nodier Medical Officer to 7/51 coy 56 Batl down Road passes of Town Head O.C	
"	26/4/19		General Routine. 8 Sick arrivals admitted to Sick line	
"	27/4/19		Capt Rammesersh S.Wk Dolion For Mallier Zn timy Renew General Routine	
"	28/4/19		Inspection of Camp by G.O.C XI Div. General Routine	
"	29/4/19		Capt Newe inspects horses of 217 Reserves of Mos Coy.	
"	30/4/19		General Routine 14 horses admitted to Sick line	
"	31/4/19		General Routine	

H.W. Newe.
Capt A & M.C.

Army Form C. 2118.

WAR DIARY
or
INTELLIGENCE SUMMARY.
(Erase heading not required.)

Place	Date	Hour	Summary of Events and Information	Remarks and references to Appendices
Berlin	17/1/19		Capt Scotty attends Veterinary Board at 2/7th R.H.A. 6 sick animals evacuated to No 1 Capt V.E.C.	
"	18/1/19		" " " " " " " " "	
"	19/1/19		" " " " " " General Routine	
"	20/1/19		" " " " 7 sick animals admitted to sick lines	
"	21/1/19		Visits XI Corps Field Cashier General Routine	
"	22/1/19		General Routine 6 sick animals evacuated to No XI Corps V.E.S.	
"	23/1/19		General Routine	
"	28/1/19		Capt Scotty visits 2/18th K.R.R. for Meeting of Mercer Mules	
"	24/1/19		" proceeds on tour to N.R. Capt Mauer takes over General Routine	
"	25/1/19		Capt Mauer Mullens Horses of M.I Coy 19 Battn sick + Lame + transferred O.R.	
"	26/1/19		General Routine 8 Horses admitted to sick lines	
"	27/1/19		Capt Mauer Visits S.a.a Section for Medical History of Horses	
"	28/1/19		Inspection of camp by G.O.C. 29 Div General Routine	
"	29/1/19		Capt Mauer inspects horses of 314 Prisoners of Military	
"	30/1/19		General Routine 14 Horses admitted to sick lines	
"	31/1/19		General Routine	

J.W. Mauer
Capt R.A.V.C

Capt A.V.M. attd. 11 Div. Rev. Section

WAR DIARY or INTELLIGENCE SUMMARY

Army Form C. 2118.

Place	Date	Hour	Summary of Events and Information	Remarks and references to Appendices
Berlin	1/2/19	9	Capt. Dawes visits 1b 513 Coy R.A.S.C. for the Men, the 3rd horses – General Routine	
"	2/2/19	9	Capt. Dawes visits 2/3 Field Amb. to review Sgt. Mallon. Capt. Pattison M.O. 2 animals admitted to sick lines	
"	3/2/19	9	General Routine. 14 animals transferred to 6 XI Coy to V.E.S.	
"	4/2/19	9	General Routine. 4 animals admitted to sick lines	
"	5/2/19	9	General Routine. Visit of D.A.D.V.S.	
"	6/2/19	9	General Routine. 4 animals transferred to 6 XI Coy to V.E.S.	
"	7/2/19	9	General Routine.	
"	8/2/19	9	General Routine. 3 Horses admitted to sick lines	
"	9/2/19	9	General Routine. Horses & action classified by Div. Remount Officer	
"	10/2/19	9	Capt. Dawes visits D.A.D. & I.M.C.O. and 5 men report to XI Coy to V.E.S. for duty	
"	11/2/19	9	General Routine	
"	12/2/19	9	Capt. Dawes visits 513 Coy R.A.S.C. to inspect horses T.M.O. & 5 men return from XI Coy V.E.S.	
"	13/2/19	9	General Routine. Ambulance collects Tower horse from West Riding H.A. R.F.A.	
"	14/2/19	9	General Routine. Ambulance collects sick mule from 277 Bde R.F.A.	
"	15/2/19	9	General Routine. 12 animals admitted to sick lines. 20 transferred to 6 XI Coy to V.E.L.	
"	16/2/19	9	Capt. Stobry reports from leave to U.K. General Routine.	

WAR DIARY or INTELLIGENCE SUMMARY

Army Form C. 2118.

Place	Date	Hour	Summary of Events and Information	Remarks and references to Appendices
Berlin	17/2/19		Capt Sorby attends sick horse at 59 Signal Coy R.E. Ambulance collects sick animal from stagnery horsp	
"	18/2/19		General Routine. 5 animals admitted to sick lines	
"	19/2/19		Capt Sorby attends funeral of Capt Bradley R.V.S. Capt Harrison 8 animals admitted 5 transferred to XI Corps V.E.S.	
"	20/2/19		General Routine. 5 animals transferred to XI Corps V.E.S and 18 admitted sick lines. General Routine	
"	21/2/19		Capt Sorby visits XI Corps Field Cashier. 18 animals transferred to XI Corps V.E.S.	
"	22/2/19		Visit of D.A.D.V.S. General Routine. 7 animals admitted to sick lines	
"	23/2/19		General Routine. Ambulance collects 7 sick horses from 296 Bde R.F.A.	
"	24/2/19		Capt Sorby visits D.A.D.V.S. at Head Quarters. 5 animals transferred to XI Corps V.E.S.	
"	25/2/19		Capt Sorby inspects animals of Berlin railhead prior to entraining to Aulnoye Base	
"	26/2/19		Capt Sorby visits 296 Bde R.F.A. 59 Div. C.S animal showing symp. Rabies & sent to Z Animals. 7 animals transferred	
"	27/2/19		Capt Sorby conducts sale at Z animals at Heaven. 9 visits XI Corps Field Cashier. 7 animals transferred	
"	28/2/19		Capt Sorby visits XI Corps Field Cashier. General Routine	

G P Sorby
Capt R.A.V.C.

WAR DIARY or INTELLIGENCE SUMMARY.

Army Form C. 2118.

Place	Date	Hour	Summary of Events and Information	Remarks and references to Appendices
Burbure	1/3/15		General Routine Visit of D.A.D.V.S. ambulance collected sick horses from 2 go Fd. Bty.	
	2/3/15		" " 6 Sick animals admitted to Sick lines	
	3/3/15		Capt Scotty visits sick animal Stony Camp Bulin nine sick horses admitted to sick lines	
	4/3/15		Capt Scotty conducts sale of 182 animals at Bruay. 4 animals admitted to sick lines	
	5/3/15		Capt Scotty visits XI Corps Field Ambulance collected 2 sick animals & removal transport	
	6/3/15		General Routine and Packing of stores	
	7/3/15		Proceed by march route to Aire	
	8/3/15		Proceed by march route to Sercues	
	9/3/15		Proceed by march route to Rebuisseau	
Rebuisseau	10/3/15		General Routine. Cleaning of Stables & fitting up of sick lines	
	11/3/15		Capt Scotty visits sick lines of 1/2 Field ambulance & 2/3 N. Midland by R.E. general routine	
	12/3/15		Capt Scotty visits A.D.V.S. at 39 Divn. Head Qtrs. General Routine	
	13/3/15		General Routine	

Army Form C. 2118.

WAR DIARY
or
INTELLIGENCE SUMMARY.
(Erase heading not required.)

Instructions regarding War Diaries and Intelligence Summaries are contained in F. S. Regs., Part II. and the Staff Manual respectively. Title pages will be prepared in manuscript.

Place	Date	Hour	Summary of Events and Information	Remarks and references to Appendices
Babingdon	14/9/15		General Routine	
"	16/9/15		"	
"	19/9/15		"	
"	20/9/15		"	
"	21/9/15		Capt. Sooty Visits Boat Supplies Calais area. General Routine	
"	20/8/15		General Routine	
"	23/9/15		Capt Sooty Visits R.V.V.S Calais 2 his	
"	24/8/15		General Routine	
"	25/8/15		"	
"	26/8/15		Capt. Sooty visits Head Qtr 55 Div & English horsed trans Headquarters 3 Div Arm d	
"	27/9/15		"	
"	28/9/15		"	
"	29/9/15		"	
"	30/9/15		Capt Sooty proceeded to Boulogne to attend D.A. Director V.S. 1st Army A.C.	
"	31/9/15		"	

Guy Rhodes Capt RAVC

WAR DIARY
or
INTELLIGENCE SUMMARY.
(Erase heading not required.)

Army Form C. 2118.

Instructions regarding War Diaries and Intelligence Summaries are contained in F. S. Regs., Part II. and the Staff Manual respectively. Title pages will be prepared in manuscript.

Place	Date	Hour	Summary of Events and Information	Remarks and references to Appendices
Babington	1/4/19		General Routine	
"	2/4/19		"	
"	3/4/19		"	
"	4/4/19		"	
"	5/4/19		"	
"	6/4/19		"	
"	7/4/19		"	
"	8/4/19		"	
"	9/4/19		"	
"	10/4/19		"	
"	11/4/19		"	
"	12/4/19		"	
"	13/4/19		"	
"	14/4/19		"	
"	15/4/19		"	
"	16/4/19		"	

Army Form C. 2118.

WAR DIARY
or
INTELLIGENCE SUMMARY.
(Erase heading not required.)

Instructions regarding War Diaries and Intelligence Summaries are contained in F. S. Regs., Part II. and the Staff Manual respectively. Title pages will be prepared in manuscript.

Place	Date	Hour	Summary of Events and Information	Remarks and references to Appendices
Bulwington	1/4/19		General Routine	
	18/4/19	"	"	
	19/4/19	"	"	
	20/4/19	"	"	
	21/4/19	"	"	
	22/4/19	"	"	
	23/4/19	"	"	
	24/4/19	"	1 Section of Stores for Evacuation to Forbes	
	25/4/19	"	4 Unserviceable Slings inspected by D.A.D.V.S. 27 Div	
	26/4/19	"	"	
	27/4/19	"	Unserviceable Slings returned to D.A.D.V.S.	
	28/4/19	"		
	29/4/19	"	1 N.C.O. & 4 men report to No 4 Coy 53 Rly Train with others on basis strength of Section	
			2 Horses transferred to Vet. Hosp. Obs 3 to train Head Qtrs 2, to 16"Fld Amb under Position & 5"F	
			No 2 Coy Cox train & 2 to No 3 Coy 59 Nor train & 3 to 4 Coy 59 Nor train	
			PD(Cavy)Capt RANC

59TH DIVISION

59TH DIVISIONAL TRAIN
FEB 1917 – ~~DEC 1918~~.
AUG. 1919

(513 TO 516 COY ASC)

AND 1916 JAN — 1916 JUN

www.ingramcontent.com/pod-product-compliance
Lightning Source LLC
Chambersburg PA
CBHW081450160426
43193CB00013B/2429